POLLUTED

In Your Own Blood

Confronting the Effects of
Generational Iniquity & Reclaiming
the Kingdom Heritage of Christ

Dr. Miracle Pettenger, Th.D

DEDICATION

This book was written in honor of my mother's life, ministry, and legacy, the late Apostle Pastor Dorene King.

As I watched the video of her 1998 deliverance workshop and read the transcripts of her bible teachings, I connected with her vision of the Biblical teachings and Christ-centered Kingdom ministry, reaching a broad audience across the globe. Though it was not fulfilled in her lifetime, God gave me the grace and privilege of carrying the apostolic mantle and running with the vision.

I bless God for the opportunity to write a book, in a sense, with my mom via her transcripts! I was her firstborn child, and as I became an adult, she became my friend. I remember when I was a little girl, I would tell her, "Mommy, I want to be like you when I grow up!" She would reply, "Miracle, I don't want you to be like me; I want you to be like Jesus!"

Though she was not perfect, I learned from her life stories and the examples she set in lessons like *How to Love God More Than Anything or Anyone*; *Follow Directions Well*, *Don't Pick Up Offences Easily*, and *How to Defend the Faith*! She showed me how to trust God in every area of my life, especially with my heart's secret intimate things.

It is with tremendous love, honor, and respect that I share the revelations, insights, and teachings God has given us. Therefore, I dedicate this book solely unto my Lord & Savior Jesus Christ for His demonstration of love in the form of the late Apostle Pastor Dorene J. Mills King.

ACKNOWLEDGMENTS

As I first give honor to God for His strength, anointing, and grace in writing this book, I would like to graciously acknowledge my father, Bishop Joseph King!

Daddy, you were the first man to love me, provide for me, and teach me what it looks like when a man truly loves God. Your years of wisdom, guidance, and early morning bedside prayers helped prepare me for life with my family, ministry, and the marketplace. Thank you for being a man of integrity and believing in the God in me. Your support has helped me accomplish this mandated assignment. I honor you and call you blessed! I love you, Daddy!

Thank you, Pastor Mary L. King. You, Charvela, and Derrick have been a true blessing as part of the King Family and the ministry of New Beginnings Apostolic Faith Ministries, Inc. I love and appreciate you all.

I bless God for my brother, Elder Joe A. King, his wife Minister Robin King, and their family for their loving prayers and support. May the favor and blessings of the Lord continue to manifest in every area of your lives, in Jesus' Name!

To all of my family – Mills, Griffy, White, King, and Pettenger, I pray that the loving comfort, unity, strength, and healing peace of God guide us into the healthy, whole, and prosperous lives that come in the knowledge and fellowship of Jesus Christ.

A special thanks to Pastor Emeritus Joyce Washington! Thank you for the years of genuine friendship towards my mother and supporting her ministry in the love and fellowship of Christ. Your mentorship, guidance, and ongoing encouragement through this journey have given me joy, strength, and hope.

I would be remiss if I did not publicly thank my husband, Tad L. Pettenger! Thank you, Handsome, for your patience and care during this process. Thank you for ensuring I didn't overwork myself and making provision for me to have the time and space to flow in the anointing of the Holy Spirit. Thank you for finding me in the Heart of God! I honor you as the head of our household, dedicated father of our three exceptional children, anointed mighty man of valor, and my friend. Love you much!

Lastly, I want to thank every person who takes the time to read this ministry book. May your heart be open to receive and apply the words of healing, deliverance, and freedom that the Holy Spirit has purposed for you through the power of God's Proceeding Word! This book was a mandated assignment for a mandated audience. You are not reading this by happenstance. This is a God-ordained moment for you to experience Him in a new and different way! Now is the day of salvation! Now is the season of your breakthrough! You are exactly where you need to be to receive healing from your past hurts, deliverance from your present bondage, and freedom to live the victorious and prosperous Kingdom life God has predestined for your future.

.

CONTENTS

PREFACE

... How I was Inspired ...

his book was inspired by the New Beginnings Apostolic Faith Ministries, Inc. Deliverance Seminar, "Birthing and Activating God's Seed in Me," taught by my mother, Pastor Dorene J. King, in March 1998, and recorded at Endtime United Church of Norfolk, VA.

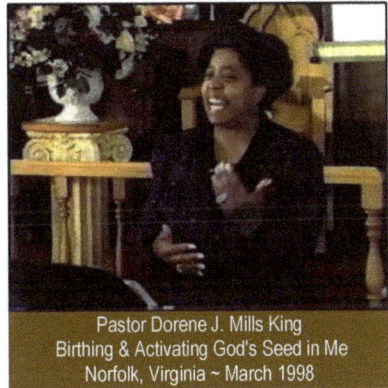

Pastor Dorene J. Mills King
Birthing & Activating God's Seed in Me
Norfolk, Virginia ~ March 1998

This conference session brought deliverance, healing, and victory to many souls. One of the fundamental truths of the conference dealt with confronting the unhealed hurts, unresolved issues, and unmet needs that paralyze the will and taunt the mind of the believer. The cause of several of our wounds is centered in the nativity of our birth. Regardless of circumstances (whether good, bad, or ugly), we must come face to face with the actions of our parents, the condition of our environments, the influence of our community, culture, social systems, and spiritual inheritance. In instances of dysfunctional and traumatic events, the iniquity of the parents results in generational curses on the offspring. Mankind was born in sin and shaped in iniquity. Therefore, the pollution of sin hinders the growth of God's pure seed planted within us.

POLLUTED IN YOUR OWN BLOOD

And the LORD God formed man of the dust of the ground,
and breathed into his nostrils the breath of life;
and man became a living soul.
Genesis 2:7 (KJV)

Behold, I was shapen in iniquity;
and in sin did my mother conceive me.
Psalm 51:5 (KJV)

For every cause, there is an effect. The polluted nativity of our births, naturally and spiritually, negatively impacts how we process information, relate to others, and view ourselves. Thankfully, God has provided a way of escape, a process of healing, and strategies to maintain recovery.

I pray this book encourages you to:

- **identify** the pollutants of dysfunctional family behaviors and belief systems,
- **purify** your spirit and soul by the direction of God's Word and committed relationship with Christ Jesus, and
- **operate** in the Kingdom heritage and prosperity of God.

INTRODUCTION

H ave you ever come to a point in your life where you just didn't know what to do? You may even begin to inquire of yourself:

"How did I end up here in this place, in this space?
Why am I not further along in my career?
How did I end up with so much debt?
How did I end up in this dysfunctional relationship?
Why does my life look like a prime-time dramatic movie?

All these questions seem to have no answers. All you really know is that you made a series of choices and decisions that led you into your current circumstances. Yet, it seems like nothing you do produces the good and godly results you believe God for. This is when we must self-examine and identify the root cause and belief systems behind our daily choices. Beliefs rooted in the wisdom of God lead to wise decisions. Whereas reckless and self-destructive beliefs lead to foolish decisions. We need to go back to the beginning and ask God to reveal the truth of our nativity, both naturally and spiritually.

Our family patterns and belief systems, or lack thereof, influence how we are nurtured, raised, and develop as individuals. This is where we see cycles of dysfunctional families producing dysfunctional children, who become dysfunctional adults. Those dysfunctional adults seek out and marry other dysfunctional adults, cultivating a society of dysfunctional individuals with destructive behaviors and irrational mindsets. Unless there is an agent of change, the cycle will perpetuate itself generation after generation.

Whether we are investigating the nativity of your family, relationships, finances, friends, or career, we can trust that the Holy Spirit will lead, guide, and direct us into all truth. This includes the truth about ourselves and our personal belief systems. The Word of God tells us all humanity was born in sin and shaped in iniquity.

> *Behold, I was brought forth in [a state of] iniquity;*
> *my mother was sinful who conceived me*
> *[and I too am sinful].*
> *Psalm 51:5 (AMPC)*

Yet the redemptive work of Christ Jesus allows us to be born again into the pure holiness of the Kingdom of God.

> *³ Jesus answered and said unto him,*
> *Verily, verily, I say unto thee, Except a man be born again,*
> *he cannot see the kingdom of God.*
> *⁴ Nicodemus saith unto him,*
> *How can a man be born when he is old?*
> *can he enter the second time*
> *into his mother's womb, and be born?*
> *⁵ Jesus answered, Verily, verily, I say unto thee,*
> *Except a man be born of water and of the Spirit,*
> *and that which is born of the Spirit is spirit.*
> *⁷ Marvel not that I said unto thee,*
> *Ye must be born again*
> *John 3:3-7 (KJV)*

Introduction

*Being **born again**, not of corruptible seed,*
but of incorruptible, by the word of God,
which liveth and abideth for ever.
1 Peter 1:23 (KJV)

Therefore, what is the current condition of your blood – your soul (mind, will, and emotions)? Is it polluted with the containments of rejection, bitterness, anger, and unforgiveness from your parents, past traumas, or previous relationships? Or have you allowed the Blood of Jesus Christ to purify every condition, whether natural, physical, mental, emotional, or spiritual? To embrace the complete heritage of the Kingdom of God, the first step is identifying the truth and confronting sin.

The Nativity of Your Birth

Chapter 1
The Circumstances of Birth

et's look at God's message to Jerusalem as He commissions the Prophet Ezekiel with a mandated assignment. The goal was to bring the following aspects to light for the nation of Israel:

1) the <u>abomination</u> of their detestable and sinful actions,
2) the truth of their spiritual and natural <u>origin</u>, and
3) their <u>nativity</u> - the circumstances and activities that took place on the day they were born.

Their Abominations ...

Ezekiel 16:1-2 (NKJV)

[1] Again the word of the Lord came to me, saying,
[2] "Son of man, cause Jerusalem to know her abominations,

God commanded the Prophet Ezekiel to cause Jerusalem to confront their abominations. But, first, they had to recognize that their actions were genuinely detestable practices and shamefully vile in the sight of God. Though many customs were socially acceptable, they were revolting attempts to usurp the authority of God. Unfortunately, in today's society, we are so accustomed to doing what is socially acceptable that many idolatrous traditions have become social norms. Yet, in the light of God's Word, they are an affront to His Holiness and righteous standards for Kingdom Living.

> *Cry aloud, spare not, lift up thy voice like a trumpet,*
> *and shew my people their transgression,*
> *and the house of Jacob their sins.*
> *Isaiah 58:1 (KJV)*

Only when we examine ourselves in the Light of God's Word can the Holy Spirit reveal the divine truth. We can then confront those sinful actions and position ourselves for Kingdom victory.

Their Origin ...

Ezekiel 16:3 (NKJV)

³ and say, 'Thus says the Lord God to Jerusalem:
"Your birth and your nativity are from the land of Canaan;
your father was an Amorite and your mother a Hittite.

The location and behavior of individuals (whether sinful or righteous) surrounding our birth can have effects. Likewise, the consequences of parental iniquity can last generations. Therefore, it matters who your mother and father are. Whether we realize it or not, the environment and the people within it impact our lives.

Their Nativity ...

Ezekiel 16:4 (NKJV)

⁴ As for your nativity, on the day you were born your navel cord
was not cut, nor were you washed in water to cleanse you;
you were not rubbed with salt nor wrapped in swaddling cloths.

Merriam Webster defines *nativity* as *"the process or circumstances of being born: BIRTH"* and *"the place of origin."*[1] Thus, the Lord shares with Ezekiel the details of the nation's birth as a newborn infant. Their umbilical cord was not cut properly. Their body was abused because it was not washed or adequately cleansed. The filth of their sin and disobedience remained and became infected. No one treated the infection with the salt of forgiveness nor wrapped them in a clean dressing to ensure healing and loving security. The caregivers' responsibilities and duties to prepare the new infant for a viable life were abandoned. The infant nation was indeed neglected. Such caregivers would have been reported to the Child Protective Services Agency for child abuse and negligence in this day and age. The inflicted wounds and trauma were not only physical but mental and emotional, causing the nation to make shameful and perverted choices as they searched for protection and acceptance in all the wrong places.

Ezekiel 16:5 (NKJV)

[5] No eye pitied you, to do any of these things for you, to have compassion on you; but you were thrown out into the open field, when you yourself were loathed on the day you were born.

The mindset of the society and the natural environment factor into the nativity as well. The neighboring people did not have pity or compassion for the infant nation. They were thrown out into an open field despised, destitute, and left to die. This response leads to a spirit of rejection, self-rejection, and rebellion.

---

[1] "Nativity." Merriam-Webster.com Dictionary, Merriam-Webster, https://www.merriam-webster.com/dictionary/nativity. Accessed 27 Jul. 2021.

Chapter 2
Defining Generational Iniquity

God has established universal laws as a way for His glory to operate in our lives spiritually and naturally. Whether we are aware of them or not, they function to carry out God's original intent and purpose. Those universal laws include the Law of Blessing and Cursing, the Law of Multiplication, the Law of Sowing and Reaping, and the Law of Generational Iniquity.[2] God's laws and promises do not change, neither do the consequences of the actions that go against His Word.

> *[19] If ye be willing and obedient,*
> *ye shall eat the good of the land:*
> *[20] But if ye refuse and rebel,*
> *ye shall be devoured with the sword:*
> *for the mouth of the Lord hath spoken it.*
> *Isaiah 1:19-20 (KJV)*

In <u>Freedom from Generational Sin</u>, author Ruth Hawkey shares the specific terms used to describe the different actions in conflict with God's will, laws, commandments, and Kingdom. Each carries clear consequences and is subject to God's universal laws. [3]

---

[2] Hawkey, Ruth. "Chapter 1 – The Laws of God." *Freedom from Generational Sin*. Chichester: New Wine Press, 1999. Book.

[3] Hawkey, Ruth. "Chapter 1 – The Laws of God." *Freedom from Generational Sin*. Chichester: New Wine Press, 1999. Book. pgs. 12-13.

➢ **Sin** – falling short; an error; a failure; an independence of God

➢ **Transgression** – the breaking of a specific rule or law

➢ **Trespass** – going onto forbidden territory; going where you shouldn't in spite of warnings and notices

➢ **Iniquity** – lawlessness; some sin or sins, resulting from a wrong desire, lawlessness, or a perverseness, which then causes a weakness and a compulsion in the make-up of our descendants or in us as a result of the sins of our ancestors.

> *Against you, you only, have I sinned*
> *and done what is evil in your sight;*
> *so you are right in your verdict*
> *and justified when you judge.*
> *Psalm 51:4 (NIV)*

When Adam and Eve broke the specific rule God gave them in the Garden of Eden (a transgression against God), they became aware of both good and evil. This caused all humanity to have a weakness and capacity to desire independence from God, i.e., a sinful nature.

Psalm 51:5 (KJV)[4]

*Behold, I was **shapen** [H2342] in **iniquity**; [H5771] and in **sin** [H2399] did my **mother** [H517] **conceive** [H3179] me.*

Let's take a closer look at the original Hebrew meanings of the terms used in Psalm 51:5 for a greater understanding of how the sinful nature of humanity produces generational iniquity.

---

[4] "Psalm 51 (KJV) - Behold, I was shapen in." Blue Letter Bible. Web. 16 Aug, 2021. <https://www.blueletterbible.org/kjv/psa/51/5/ss1/s_529005>.

14

Strong's Hebrew Lexicon (KJV) Definitions
for Psalm 51:5

shapen; Strong's H2342 - ḥûl [5]
חוּל *chûwl, khool; or* חִיל *chîyl; a primitive root; properly, to twist or whirl (in a circular or spiral manner), i.e. (specifically) to dance, to writhe in pain (especially of parturition) or fear; figuratively, to wait, to pervert:—bear, (make to) bring forth, (make to) calve, dance, drive away, fall grievously (with pain), fear, form, great, grieve, (be) grievous, hope, look, make, be in pain, be much (sore) pained, rest, shake, shapen, (be) sorrow(-ful), stay, tarry, travail (with pain), tremble, trust, wait carefully (patiently), be wounded.*

iniquity; Strong's H5771 - ʿāôn [6]
עָוֹן *ʿâvôn, aw-vone'; or* עָווֹן *ʿâvôwn; (2 Kings 7:9; Psalm 51:5 [7]), from H5753; perversity, i.e. (moral) evil:—fault, iniquity, mischeif, punishment (of iniquity), sin.*

sin; Strong's H2399 - ḥēṭ' [7]
חֵטְא *chêṭeʾ, khate; from H2398; a crime or its penalty:—fault, × grievously, offence, (punishment of) sin.*

conceive; Strong's H3179 - yāḥam [8]
יָחַם *yâcham, yaw-kham'; a primitive root; probably to be hot; figuratively, to conceive:—get heat, be hot, conceive, be warm.*

---

[5] "H2342 - ḥûl - Strong's Hebrew Lexicon (kjv)." Blue Letter Bible. Web. 16 Aug, 2021

[6] "H5771 - ʿāôn - Strong's Hebrew Lexicon (kjv)." Blue Letter Bible. Web. 16 Aug, 2021.

[7] "H2399 - ḥēṭ' - Strong's Hebrew Lexicon (kjv)." Blue Letter Bible. Web. 16 Aug, 2021.

[8] "H3179 - yāḥam - Strong's Hebrew Lexicon (kjv)." Blue Letter Bible. Web. 16 Aug, 2021.

mother; *Strong's H517 -' ēm* [9]

אֵם *'êm, ame; a primitive word; a mother (<u>as the bond of the</u> <u>family</u>); in a wide sense (both literally and figuratively [like father]):—dom, mother, × parting.*

The author shares that the sinful nature of mankind was willfully made *(shapen)* by perverse desires *(iniquity)* and developed through a process *(conceived)* of offensive acts against the Sovereign God *(sin)* by his ancestorial composition *(mother)*.

Humanity's need to be independent of God rather than dependent on Him opened the door for selfish lusts and self-gratifying behaviors. **Generational iniquity** is the compulsive desire to demonstrate independence from God by surrendering to the selfish desires and actions that perversely offend His character, nature, and image.

Behold, thou desirest truth in the inward parts:
and in the hidden part thou shalt make me to know wisdom.
Psalm 51:6 (KJV)

---

[9] "H517 - 'ēm - Strong's Hebrew Lexicon (kjv)." Blue Letter Bible. Web. 16 Aug, 2021.

Chapter 3
Defining Generational Curse

²⁶ Behold, I set before you this day a blessing and a curse;
²⁷ A blessing, if ye obey the commandments of the Lord
your God, which I command you this day:
²⁸ And a curse, if ye will not obey the commandments of the
Lord your God, but turn aside out of the way
which I command you this day, to go after other gods,
which ye have not known.
Deuteronomy 11:26-28 (KJV)

A generational curse is the result of unrepented *generational iniquity.* Humanity has habitually turned away from God's universal laws through sin, transgressions, trespasses, and iniquities. These disobedient actions introduce family flaws and weaknesses passed from generation to generation, opening doors for perverse addictions, sickness, and curses within the family system. Consequently, future generations become vulnerable to sinning in the same areas (addictions, sexual abuse, violence) and compound the problem within the family line.

Thou shalt not bow down thyself to them, nor serve them:
for I the LORD thy God am a jealous God,
visiting the iniquity of the fathers upon the children
unto the third and fourth generation of them that hate me;
Exodus 20:5 (KJV)

During the 1998 Deliverance Seminar, "Birthing & Activating God's Seed in Me," presented by NBAFM, Inc., Pastor Dorene J. King gave revelatory insight (based on Ezekiel 16:1-5) on the relationship between the nativity and generational curses referencing a medical diagram of a newborn birthed with a disease.

> ... looking at the significance of where the mother came from. Scripture says that your father was an Amorite and your mother was a Hittite. Why is it important to know the history, generational ancestral history, nativity, circumstances, and situation around our birth? This transparency shows you a baby. The umbilical cord is still connected to the baby, but this baby has syphilis. The patches on the newborn represent syphilis.
>
> There were many things that we do not get straight, ... we are born with different spiritual sicknesses and diseases. Now, that baby was just born, so that baby didn't go have sex and get syphilis. Syphilis was a generational curse. Syphilis came from the mother, the father, whatever [the circumstance may have been]. It came down the line, but that baby can be cleaned up. That baby can be cleaned up and be healthy.
>
> ... Pastor Dorene J. King

A **Generational curse** is the established judgment and generational consequences for those who choose to violate the commandments and laws of God. It leads a person or family to a place where they can acknowledge their faults, recognize their need for a Savior and Lord, ask and receive the mercy and forgiveness of God, and live in the freedom of God.

> [18] *'The Lord is longsuffering and abundant in mercy,*
> *forgiving iniquity and transgression;*
> **but He by no means clears the guilty,**
> **visiting the iniquity** *of the fathers on the children*
> *to the third and fourth generation.'*
> [19] **Pardon the iniquity of this people,**
> **I pray,** *according to the greatness of Your mercy,*
> **just as You have forgiven this people,**
> *from Egypt even until now."*
> [20] *Then the Lord said:* **"I have pardon ed,'**
> **according to your w ord;'**
> *Numbers 14:18-20 (NKJV)*

Pollution

Chapter 4
The Dysfunctional Family

E very family system is impacted by generational curses in some form or fashion. Our families are where we first learn about ourselves. Our core identity comes from the mirroring eyes of our caretakers. There are two types of family patterns that exist, as described by Dr. Russell R. Kopp.[10]

> ➢ *CONSTRUCTIVE family patterns produce* **HEALTHY** *or* **FUNCTIONAL** *family systems. This is a family that is functioning properly and is providing the necessary elements that will promote the growth of its members into all that God has created them to become.*
>
> ➢ *DESTRUCTIVE family patterns produce* **UNHEALTHY** *or* **DYSFUNCTIONAL** *family systems. This family cannot function properly and is causing the members to be stunted in their growth (emotionally and spiritually) and is forcing the members to be what the system needs them to become.*

If the family is dysfunctional, then the children are viewed as instruments to sustain and maintain the system into the next generation. Dysfunctional parents create dysfunctional patterns in their children, producing dysfunctional children. Dysfunctional

---

[10] Kopp, Dr. Russell R. "Chapter 2: The Family as a System – Two General Types of Family." An Introduction to Family Systems: A Study of the Family as a System and How to Create a Healthy Family System. Jacksonville: Logos, n.d. Text Book. pgs 15-16.

children grow up to become dysfunctional adults. Dysfunctional adults marry and create dysfunctional families, perpetuating the cycle. But there is hope!

We can find examples of generational iniquity in the Bible, ranging from sexual sins, dishonor, and deceit to murder and idolatry. For example, the family line of Abraham, Isaac, and Jacob reveals a familial trait of the husbands' self-centered justification for exposing their wives to possible sexual abuse.

Genesis 12:11-13 (NLT)

[11] As he was approaching the border of Egypt, Abram said to his wife, Sarai, "Look, you are a very beautiful woman.
[12] When the Egyptians see you, they will say, 'This is his wife. Let's kill him; then we can have her!'
[13] So please tell them you are my sister. Then they will spare my life and treat me well because of their interest in you."

In Genesis Chapter 12, we see Abram engaging in a shared social practice of the time. He forced Sarai into claiming to be his sister rather than his wife out of fear that the Egyptians would kill her husband to obtain Sarai for their own perverse sexual pleasures. As if to say, the same God who told Abram to leave his father's house would not be able to protect him and his wife along the journey. Unfortunately, Abram chooses to make his fear of man greater than his faith in God. He continues to cling to this dysfunctional rational as he travels through Egypt.

Genesis 20:1-2 (NLT) ... Abraham Deceives Abimelech

[1]Abraham moved south to the Negev and lived for a while between Kadesh and Shur, and then he moved on to Gerar. While living there as a foreigner, [2]Abraham introduced his wife, Sarah, by saying, "She is my sister." So King Abimelech

of Gerar sent for Sarah and had her brought to him at his palace.

When living in Gerar, Abraham chooses to forsake his covenant oath to protect Sarah and, in essence, willingly prostituted his wife to save his own life. In Genesis 20:3, we see that God intervenes before Sarah is compromised and reveals the true nature of Abraham's relationship with her to King Abimelech. This foreign king was willing to honor the truth of the One True and Living God, even when Abraham, the one whom God made a covenant promise, was not.

This deceptive and self-centered mentality was transmitted down Abraham's family line to the next generation. His son, Isaac, made the same self-serving choice concerning his wife, Rebekah, while in the same land of Gerar, as mentioned in Genesis Chapter 26.

Genesis 26:6-7 (NLT)

[6] So Isaac stayed in Gerar.

[7] When the men who lived there asked Isaac about his wife, Rebekah, he said, "She is my sister." He was afraid to say, "She is my wife." He thought, "They will kill me to get her, because she is so beautiful."

Isaac followed the dysfunctional pattern and belief system his father modeled for him. He responded dishonestly, just as Abraham, stating that Rebekah was his sister in fear of his life, rather than trusting God to protect him and his wife. Isaac's learned behavior made Rebekah eligible for sexual exploitation in a foreign land. Thankfully, God allowed King Abimelech of the Philistines to see the truth with his own eyes and protected Rebekah from danger, as seen in Genesis 26:8-11.

Genesis 26:8-11 (NLT)

⁸ But some time later, Abimelech, king of the Philistines, looked out his window and saw Isaac caressing Rebekah.

⁹ Immediately, Abimelech called for Isaac and exclaimed, "She is obviously your wife! Why did you say, 'She is my sister'?"

"Because I was afraid someone would kill me to get her from me," Isaac replied.

¹⁰ "How could you do this to us?" Abimelech exclaimed. "One of my people might easily have taken your wife and slept with her, and you would have made us guilty of great sin."

¹¹ Then Abimelech issued a public proclamation: "Anyone who touches this man or his wife will be put to death!"

In the third generation, the same dysfunctional pattern of marital deceit manifests with different behaviors. It was Abraham's grandson, Jacob, who was manipulated into a marriage with Leah after Laban initially promised him the hand of Rachel. The bitterness and resentment in Jacob's heart transferred into his marital relations with Leah, affecting her physically, emotionally, and mentally.

Genesis 29:31-34 (NLT)

³¹ When the Lord saw that Leah was unloved, he enabled her to have children, but Rachel could not conceive. ³² So Leah became pregnant and gave birth to a son. She named him Reuben, for she said, "The Lord has noticed my misery, and now my husband will love me."

³³ She soon became pregnant again and gave birth to another son. She named him Simeon, for she said, "The Lord heard that I was unloved and has given me another son."

³⁴ Then she became pregnant a third time and gave birth to another son. He was named Levi, for she said, "Surely this time my husband will feel affection for me, since I have given him three sons!"

Jacob was so focused on his agenda to wed Rachel that he mistreated his wife Leah with contempt and was blind to the hatred he inflicted on her soul. Yet, God saw her unmet needs for love and acceptance from her husband and responded in love by blessing her womb with children.

Even in the family line of Abraham, Isaac, and Jacob, we see that the curse of unrepented iniquity can travel from one generation to the next when God-centered patterns are not in place to promote healthy social relationships and an authentic spiritual connection with God.

Chapter 5
Destructive Patterns & Poison Fruit

Natural Comes before Spiritual

And the Lord God formed man of the dust of the ground,
and breathed into his nostrils the breath of life;
and man became a living soul.
Genesis 2:7 (KJV)

What comes first is the natural body,
then the spiritual body comes later.
1 Corinthians 15:46 (NLT)

In this excerpt, Pastor King reminds us that we must face the facts about ourselves. Just as we learned in Genesis 2:7 that God first formed man from the dust of the ground and then breathed the life into him to become a living soul, we must understand how the natural symptoms have a spiritual connection.

> *The question came up, ... "Why do we have to deal with the things in the natural?" Because natural comes before spiritual. There's a connection there. We have got to deal with what happens to us naturally. Then we will understand what is happening to us spiritually.*
>
> *Every sin, everything that we do in the natural has a spiritual root. You're not misbehaving or being rebellious just because. There is a spiritual root to that*

natural rebellion. There was a spiritual root to that perverted sex. There's a spiritual root to why you want people to pay attention to you. Why do you have to be the center of attention? There's a spiritual root to that. My God!

... Pastor Dorene J. King

The enemy will do anything to prevent you from identifying the natural issues and overcoming the spiritual roots of iniquity in your life. He will try to discourage and torment you, but thanks be to God who gives us the victory and has all power!

Prophetic Prayer to Prepare for Deliverance

We come against every foul and hindering spirit that will block the ears of the people so that they will not hear. Satan, we give you and your demons, your walking papers, now in the Name of Jesus! We release ourselves into the presence of God and under the Blood of Jesus that we will have peace in God to deal with these sensitive issues in the presence of God, the Holy Spirit. God, He is a safe place for us. And you will not hinder us from receiving what God has. I can see the demons as I stand here, trying to hinder some of you from receiving. I can see it, but I see the Angels encamp round about you right now. [heavenly language] I see the Angels; they're warring over you right now! [heavenly language]. They want you to have peace in who you are, in the very essence of your being. My God, my God, my God. We're gonna get this!

... Pastor Dorene J. King

> *46 Howbeit that was not first which is spiritual,*
> *but that which is natural; and afterward that*
> *which is spiritual. 47 The first man is of the earth, earthy;*
> *the second man is the Lord from heaven.*
> *1 Corinthians 15:46 -47 (KJV)*

Know Your Abominations

If you want to know your abominations, you must be willing to allow God to expose the secret things of your heart. Therefore, Pastor King encourages believers to allow God to reveal the spiritual root.

"Again, the word of the Lord came unto me saying son of man, cause Jerusalem to know her abominations." [Ezekiel 16:1-2]

God wants you to know your abominations. *He wants you to know what's bothering you. Hallelujah. God, why do we have so many secrets? Why do we have so many secrets? Why? Because* ***sometimes, we think secrecy can hide sin, but secrecy doesn't hide sin. God exposes the secret things. He digs deep.***

God wants us to know our abominations. The things that are not pleasing God. We must please God if we're going to cleanse ourselves. Cleanse our spirit and our flesh and live unto wholeness and perfect a Holy way of life. We must release God. Give God permission to release Himself in us and stop releasing everything else in yourself.

... Pastor Dorene J. King

Giving God permission to release His healing presence within us requires complete transparency about the issues we tend to hide from ourselves and others. The enemy wants to deceive believers into thinking that revealing those secrets to God will make them vulnerable and weak. When honestly, it only keeps them in the bondage of mental torment, bitterness, resentment, self-rejection, rebellion, and unforgiveness. True peace and freedom comes when we allow the Holy Spirit to reveal the hidden issues and strengthen us on the journey towards healing and victory.

In this excerpt, Pastor King openly shares her process of confronting her own family's abominations and sexual abuse that she experienced as a child.

> *The White Snow Suit*
>
> *My earliest memory of a child is walking to my mom's front porch. My mom lives on a hill. [I was] walking to my mom's front porch, down a dirt road in a snowsuit. And I go to the house, and my snowsuit is ripped down like that.*
>
> *I can share this all with you because I went to each one of these people and told them I was writing the book and going to preach about it. So if they heard their name, get over it! I sure did! I went right to Parkesburg, Pennsylvania; Coatesville, Pennsylvania; Atglen, Pennsylvania, and talked to my relatives and told them, "I remember what you did to me!" My uncle is 87 years old. I sat his wife down with him, and I told him, "I remember what you did." And my aunt looked at me. She said, "He didn't do it. Oh, he wouldn't do that." But come to find out, he also tried to assault two of my*

sisters, and he assaulted his own daughter, but I was the only one that spoke it out. But see, I know God had called me to that. My husband had told me a while ago, "God has called you; [God] has called you with a ministry to reach in an area that a lot of people have not been called to reach." And see, I'm not afraid. I am not afraid or ashamed of the gospel of Jesus Christ. And I'm not afraid of the work that God has done in me because it's for the benefit of the body. I got free. And I want you to be free.

I walked to the porch in a snowsuit, and my snowsuit was ripped. I got in the house, and my mom, I must've been about six or seven years old; might've been five, and my mom said, "What happened?" and I went forth to tell her what happened. Well, they thought it was a neighbor boy from down the road. At that time, the police chief guy's name was Carl Henry. So they call Carl Henry, and the police chief guy came up, and they took a report, and they went down to the guy's house and proceeded to arrest him, this, that, and the other. Come to find out, it was not the man down the street. It was my uncle that lived two houses up. And we dealt with that. Now that experience laid dormant in my mind and my subconscious.

In 1987, my mother came to visit us in California. Before she came, I was having dreams about being, uh, as a child being molested. And I kept saying, "Well, I'm watching too much stuff on TV." And it kept coming back, it kept coming back, kept coming back. I wasn't too much into this inner healing and all that *stuff. Cause it wasn't prominent in the church back then. I wasn't in it. But this dream kept coming to me. So when my mom came to visit, I shared that with her, and she said, "Dorene, that is not a dream." And I said, "What do you mean?" She said, "Don't you remember when you came in the house, and you were crying and your clothes, your snowsuit was ripped off of you. And we thought it was the boy down the street, but it was your uncle that had molested you."*

I had pushed that thing back so far that I thought it was a dream, but when it came to the surface, God healed me. He began the healing process. I began to learn how to cut that cord of that thing. I began to learn that a lot of my feelings of low self-esteem and no self-esteem came from a feeling of rejection and feeling that I must've did something to deserve it.

And then the cap of my healing was when I had moved. I moved here, and it was the first year that we were here, and I had the Secret Closet [Outreach and] Prayer [Ministry] on Collie Avenue. And we were feeding the hungry that year for Thanksgiving. And I had went to Pennsylvania to get canned goods and everything. I was sitting in my mom's house. I said, "I'll be right back." I walked down the dirt road, two houses up, knocked on the door, told my aunt, "Hi. Uh, I like to talk to you and uncle." And she said, "About what?" I said, "I got two things, something serious and something that's pleasurable." So they sat down, and they [were] 80 some years old. I said, "the first thing is the serious thing." I said, "I remember that you molested me when

I was a child, and I'm not going to hell over bitterness behind what you did. And I am going to forgive you because it is a choice. I choose to forgive you." Well, my aunt, she denied it. And I looked at my uncle. I said, "Did you not do it?" She looked at him and said, "Deny it! Deny it!" But he would never deny it. He would never deny [it]. He just shook his head like this. I said, "You did it. I remember, and I'm not going to hell behind bitterness behind this because my marriage is healed. My sexual relationship with my husband is healed. And I am not carrying this mess because I'm writing a book, and I'm going to preach this. And I'm telling the body of Christ. So, I thought I'd let you know before you see it on TV. Before you see it, I thought I'll let you know."

We got healed! But do you see, that was over me. And because even though I did not, a child between five and seven years old, I didn't ask my uncle to molest me, to put his hands on me. He made the little girl sit on his lap while he took his private parts and did what he wanted. He used his fingers and did what he wanted. We need to speak to our children. We need to get an understanding of what's going on. When they come to us, we need to stop brushing them off. I thank God. My mom didn't brush me off. Hallelujah. These are the type of things that cause us to be unbalanced, saved adults.

... Pastor Dorene J. King

No longer can we go day to day ignoring the dysfunctional effects and symptoms that negatively impact our lives. To confront the impact of unhealed hurts, unmet needs, and unresolved issues, we must identify the natural fruit and trace it to the spiritual root.

Let us take time to examine the nature and understand the damaging effects of unhealed hurts, unmet needs, and unresolved issues.

Unhealed Hurts

The trials, tribulations, and unexpected hardships of life can cause trauma and painful wounds when not treated with the healing virtue of God's Word.

WEBSTER'S DEFINITION OF HURT

Definition of **HURT** - *noun*[11]

1: a cause of injury or damage

2a: a bodily injury or wound

b: mental or emotional distress or anguish : SUFFERING (*getting past the hurt of a bitter divorce*)

3: WRONG, HARM

SCRIPTURE REFERENCES ON HURT

*Let them be confounded and put to shame that seek after my soul: let them be turned back and brought to confusion that **devise my hurt**.*
Psalm 35:4 (KJV)

---

[11]"Hurt." Merriam-Webster.com Dictionary, Merriam-Webster, https://www.merriam-webster.com/dictionary/hurt. Accessed 16 Aug. 2021.

Let them be ashamed and brought to confusion together
*that **rejoice at mine hurt**:*
let them be clothed with shame
and dishonour that magnify themselves against me.
Psalm 35:26 (KJV)

They also that seek after my life lay snares for me:
*and **they that seek my hurt** speak mischievous things,*
and imagine deceits all the day long.
Psalm 38:12 (KJV)

STRONG'S DEFINITION OF HURT

Psalm 35:4, 26; 38:12 – hurt
Lexicon: Strong'sH7451 - ra´¹²
רַע *ra', rah; from H7489; bad or (as noun) evil (natural or moral):—adversity, affliction, calamity, displease(-ure), distress, evil((-favouredness), man or thing. , + exceedingly, × great, grief(-vous), harm, heavy, hurt(-ful), ill (favoured), + mark, mischief(-vous), misery, naught(-ty), noisome, + not please, sad(-ly), sore, sorrow, trouble, vex, wicked(-ly, -ness, one), worse(-st), wretchedness, wrong.*

EXAMPLES OF HURT

- Negative Word Curses; Demeaning Remarks, Microaggressions
- Physical Sickness and Disease
- Abuse – Physical Violence, Mental Torment, Emotional Trauma

---

[12] "H7451 - ra' - Strong's Hebrew Lexicon (kjv)." Blue Letter Bible. Web. 16 Aug, 2021.

*[2] Have mercy upon me, O Lord; for **I am weak**:*
*O Lord, heal me; for **my bones are vexed.***
***My soul is also sore vexed**: but thou, O Lord, how long?*
Psalm 6:2-3 (KJV)

*[2] Have compassion on me, Lord, for **I am weak.***
*Heal me, Lord, for **my bones are in agony.***
*[3] **I am sick at heart.***
How long, O Lord, until you restore me?
Psalm 6:2-3 (NLT)

What other examples can you think of?

_____

_____

_____

_____

NEGATIVE EFFECTS ON YOUR SOUL

Unhealed Hurts can cause you to lose sight of who you are, to the point that you can no longer see yourself the way God sees you.

- **MIND** – confusion, low self-esteem, depression; alters the way you think about yourself; distorted perception of one's image and identity
- **EMOTIONS** – pity, rejection, bitterness, anger, resentment, unforgiveness
- **WILL** – rebellion against God, isolation from others

The rape of Tamar, David's daughter, by her half-brother Amnon.

> *¹⁸ And she had a garment of divers colours upon her:*
> *for with such robes were the king's daughters that were*
> *virgins apparelled. Then his servant **brought her out,***
> *and **bolted the door after her**.*

> *¹⁹ And **Tamar put ashes on her head**, and **rent her garment***
> ***of divers colours** that was on her,*
> *and **laid her hand on her head**, and went on **crying**.*
> *2 Samuel 13:18-19 (KJV)*

If we do not allow our mind, will, and emotions to abide in the presence of the Lord, we are destined to repeat the destructive cycles that result in unhealed hurts.

Unmet Needs

Often as human beings, we do not know the difference between our wants and needs. When we allow our carnal flesh to pursue self-centered wants, we neglect the godly needs and end up in a valley of lack, poverty, and despair. Yet, when we diligently seek the Kingdom of God, the supernatural provision of God fulfills every need that pertains to life and godliness, and we abide in the green pastures flowing with milk and honey.

WEBSTER'S DEFINITION OF NEED[13]

Definition of **NEED** - *noun*

1: necessary duty : OBLIGATION

2a: **a lack of something requisite, desirable, or useful**

---

[13] "Need." Merriam-Webster.com Dictionary, Merriam-Webster, https://www.merriam-webster.com/dictionary/need. Accessed 16 Aug. 2021.

2b: a **physiological or psychological requirement for the well-being of an organism** *(such as health and education needs)*

3: a **condition requiring supply or relief** *(such as the house is in need of repair or refugees in need of shelter and food)*

4: lack of the means of subsistence: POVERTY
(The community program provides for those in need.)

SCRIPTURE REFERENCES ON NEED

*But my **God shall supply all your need**
according to his riches in glory by Christ Jesus.
Philippians 4:19 (KJV)*

*And this same God who takes care of me
will supply all **your needs** from his glorious riches,
which have been given to us in Christ Jesus.
Philippians 4:19 (NLT)*

STRONG'S DEFINITION OF NEED

Philippians 4:19 (KJV) – needs
Lexicon:: S trong'sG 5532 – chreía [14]
χρεία chreía, khri'-ah; from the base of G5530 or G5534; employment, i.e. an affair; also (by implication) occasion, demand, requirement or destitution:—business, lack, necessary(-ity), need(-ful), use, want.

---

[14] "G5532 - chreia - Strong's Greek Lexicon (kjv)." Blue Letter Bible. Web. 16 Aug, 2021.

EXAMPLES OF NEEDS

- Educational – Lack of Skills, Knowledge
- Mental – Lack of Clarity, Focus; Double-Minded; Valley of Indecision
- Emotional Instability
- Financial – Lack of Inheritance, Sustainable Income
- Physical – Improper Bodily Functions
- Material – Lack of Food, Clothing, Shelter
- Social – Lack of Companionship, Community, Family, Friends
- Spiritual – Need for Salvation, Peace, Victory for Every Attack of Weariness and Torment

[24] *"**No one can serve two masters**. For you will hate one and love the other; you will be devoted to one and despise the other. You cannot serve God and be enslaved to money.*

[25] *"That is why I tell you not to **worry about everyday life**— whether you have **enough food and drink**, or **enough clothes to wear**. Isn't life more than food, and your body more than clothing?* [26] *Look at the birds. They don't plant or harvest or store food in barns, for your heavenly Father feeds them. **Andare n'ty oufarmore valuable to him than they are?***
[27] *Can all **your worries** add a single moment to your life?*

[28] *"And why **worry about your clothing**? Look at the lilies of the field and how they grow. They don't work or make their clothing,* [29] *yet Solomon in all his glory was not dressed as beautifully as they are.* [30] *And if God cares so wonderfully for wildflowers that are here today and thrown into the fire tomorrow, he will certainly care for you. **Why do you have so little faith?***

41

³¹ *"So don't **worry about these things, saying,**
'Whatw ill wee at?Wh atw illw edri nk?Wh atw illw e wear?'*
³² *These things dominate **the thoughts of unbelievers,** but
your heavenly Father already knows all your needs.*
³³ *Seek the Kingdom of God above all else, and live
righteously, and **he will give you everything you need.***
³⁴ *"So don't worry about tomorrow, for tomorrow will bring
its own worries. Today's trouble is enough for today.*
Matthew 6:24-34 (NLT)

What other examples can you think of?

_____

_____

_____

_____

NEGATIVE EFFECTS ON YOUR SOUL?

Unmet Needs can draw focus, time, attention, and energy away from the True Source, Jehovah Jireh, and towards self-serving tactics of the enemy that lead to self-righteousness and stepping out of a relationship with the One True and Living God.

- **MIND** – stubborn, leaning to your own understanding, and refusing to acknowledge the authority of God.
- **EMOTIONS** – worrying, faithless, complaining, anxious, resentful, disappointed, fearful, unbelieving, doubting God's ability to provide; low self-worth.
- **WILL** – rebellious against the Word of God, disobedient

Unto a land flowing with milk and honey:
*for **I will not go up in the midst of thee;***
***for thou art a stiffnecked people:** lest I consume thee in the way.*
Exodus 33:3 (KJV)

Go up to this land that flows with milk and honey.
But I will not travel among you,
for you are a stubborn and rebellious people.
If I did, I would surely destroy you along the way."
Exodus 33:3 (NLT)

Unresolved Issues

Amid life's adversities and unpredictable storms, if we do not operate in the divine wisdom and discernment of God, we will not respond according to the character and integrity of His Word. Instead, we will find ourselves struggling with the internal turmoil and chaos of unresolved issues.

WEBSTER'S DEFINITION OF ISSUE

Definition of **ISSUE** - noun[15]
: a **vital or unsettled matter economic issues**
: **CONCERN, PROBLEM;** *I have issues with his behavior*
: **a matter that is in dispute between two or more parties**
: the point at which **an unsettled matter is ready for a decision;** *brought the matter to an issue*
: **a discharge (as of Blood) from the body**
: under discussion or in dispute
: **in a state of controversy: in disagreement**

---

[15] "Issue." Merriam-Webster.com Dictionary, Merriam-Webster, https://www.merriam-webster.com/dictionary/issue. Accessed 16 Aug. 2021.

SCRIPTURE REFERENCES ON ISSUES

> [5] *And now thy two sons, Ephraim and Manasseh,*
> *which were born unto thee in the land of Egypt*
> *before I came unto thee into Egypt, are mine;*
> *as Reuben and Simeon, they shall be mine.*
> [6] *And **thy issue**, which thou begettest after them,*
> *shall be thine, and shall be called*
> *after the name of their brethren in their inheritance.*
> *Genesis 48:5-6 (KJV)*

> *Keep thy heart with all diligence;*
> *for out of it are **the issues of life**.*
> *Proverbs 4:23 (KJV)*

> *And a woman having **an issue of Blood** twelve years,*
> *which had spent all her living upon physicians,*
> *neither could be healed of any,*
> *Luke 8:43 (KJV)*

STRONG'S DEFINITION OF ISSUES

Genesis 48:5-6 (KJV) – issue
Lexicon:: S trong'sH4138 – mowledeth [16]
מֹולֶדֶת *môwledeth, mo-leh'-deth; from H3205; nativity (plural birth-place); by implication, lineage, native country; also offspring, family:—begotten, born, issue, kindred, native(-ity).*

Proverbs 4:23 (KJV) – issue
Lexicon:: S trong'sH8444 - towtsa'ah [17]
תֹּוצָאָה ·tôwtsâ'âh, to-tsaw-aw'; or תֹּצָאָה ·tôtsâ'âh; from H3318; (only in plural collective) exit, i.e. (geographical) boundary,

---

[16] "H4138 - môleḏeṯ - Strong's Hebrew Lexicon (kjv)." Blue Letter Bible. Web. 16 Aug, 2021.

[17] "H8444 - tôṣā'ôṯ - Strong's Hebrew Lexicon (kjv)." Blue Letter Bible. Web. 16 Aug, 2021.

or *(figuratively)* <u>*deliverance,*</u> *(actively) source:—border(-s),*
going(-s) forth (out), <u>*issues,*</u> <u>*outgoings.*</u>

Luke 8:43 (KJV) - issue
Lexicon:: S trong'sG 4511 – rhysis [18]
ῥύσις rhýsis, hroo'-sis; from G4506 in the sense of its
congener G4482; <u>*a flux (of Blood)*</u>*:—issue.*

EXAMPLES OF UNRESOLVED ISSUES:

- Unexpected Challenges and Hardships such as Traumatic Events, Death, Financial Crisis, Sickness & Disease, Mental/Emotional Instability
- Broken & Dysfunctional Marital, Family, Social Relationships such as Family Abuse, Drama, Divorce, Betrayal, Miscommunications, Misunderstandings.
- Generational Curses, Additions, Dysfunctional Habits

What other examples can you think of?

_____

_____

_____

_____

NEGATIVE EFFECTS ON YOUR SOUL

The Unresolved Issues that may come from broken relationships, unexpected hardships, traumatic events, or generational curses can cause continual instability in the mind, chaotic emotions, unrest in spirit, and promote destructive

---

[18] "G4511 - rhysis - Strong's Greek Lexicon (kjv)." Blue Letter Bible. Web. 16 Aug, 2021.

behaviors through the action of the will.

- **MIND** – confusion, chaotic thinking, unjust suspicion, self-centered/self-righteous, uncertain
- **EMOTIONS** – rejection, resentment, anger, bitterness, unforgiveness, mistrust, pride, hopeless
- **WILL** – rebellion, disobedience, isolation, disunity, dysfunctional choices, destructive behavior

> *24 But the ship was now **in the midst of the sea,** **tossed with waves: for the wind was contrary.***
> *{the disciples were in trouble in the boat Jesus told them to get in, and **they were fighting heavy waves.***
> *Jesus comes to them walking on the water}*
> *Matthew 14:24 (KJV)*

> *2 Son of man, **thou dwellest in the midst of a rebellious house,** which have eyes to see, and **see not;** they have ears to hear, and **hear not:** for **they are a rebellious house.***
> *Ezekiel 12:2 (KJV)*

Generational Spirits & Demons Influences

What spiritual sickness or diseases are you suffering from? Generational curses can manifest in many ways, such as demonic spirits of alcoholism, drug addiction, poverty, stealing, lying, violence, child molestation, promiscuity, mental illness, fear, feelings of inferiority, suicide, as well as many diseases.

The issues listed below are often signals of a generational curse working in the bloodline[19]:

- Patterns of mental and or emotional breakdowns. (i.e., anxiety, depression, bipolar, etc.)
- Chronic sickness from a particular affliction
- Women miscarrying or not able to get pregnant.
- Family/marriage breakdowns prevalent
- Poverty / bankruptcy common
- Frequent "accidents"
- Family history of suicides or untimely deaths

> *What type of geographical demons hover over the country where your family was born? What type of demonic influences has your family been under from generation to generation to generation? I know one of the things in my family is obesity. There's a reason people overeat, and it's a demon. It's a spirit. Obesity is a spirit, and it's not just because we're hungry. You got to get control of that and break that. Diabetes, different sicknesses, different diseases.*
>
> *... Pastor Dorene J. King*

Now that you have identified the natural fruit, allow the Holy Spirit to show you the spiritual root. Then, God can pluck up what He has not planted in your life, and only His good seed will remain.

---

[19] Ibbitson, Don. "Generational Curses at Work: What are the Signs?" Christian Deliverance Ministry. *Above & Beyond Christian Counseling*, https://AandBcounseling.com/generational-curses-demonic-oppression/. Accessed 6 June 2021.

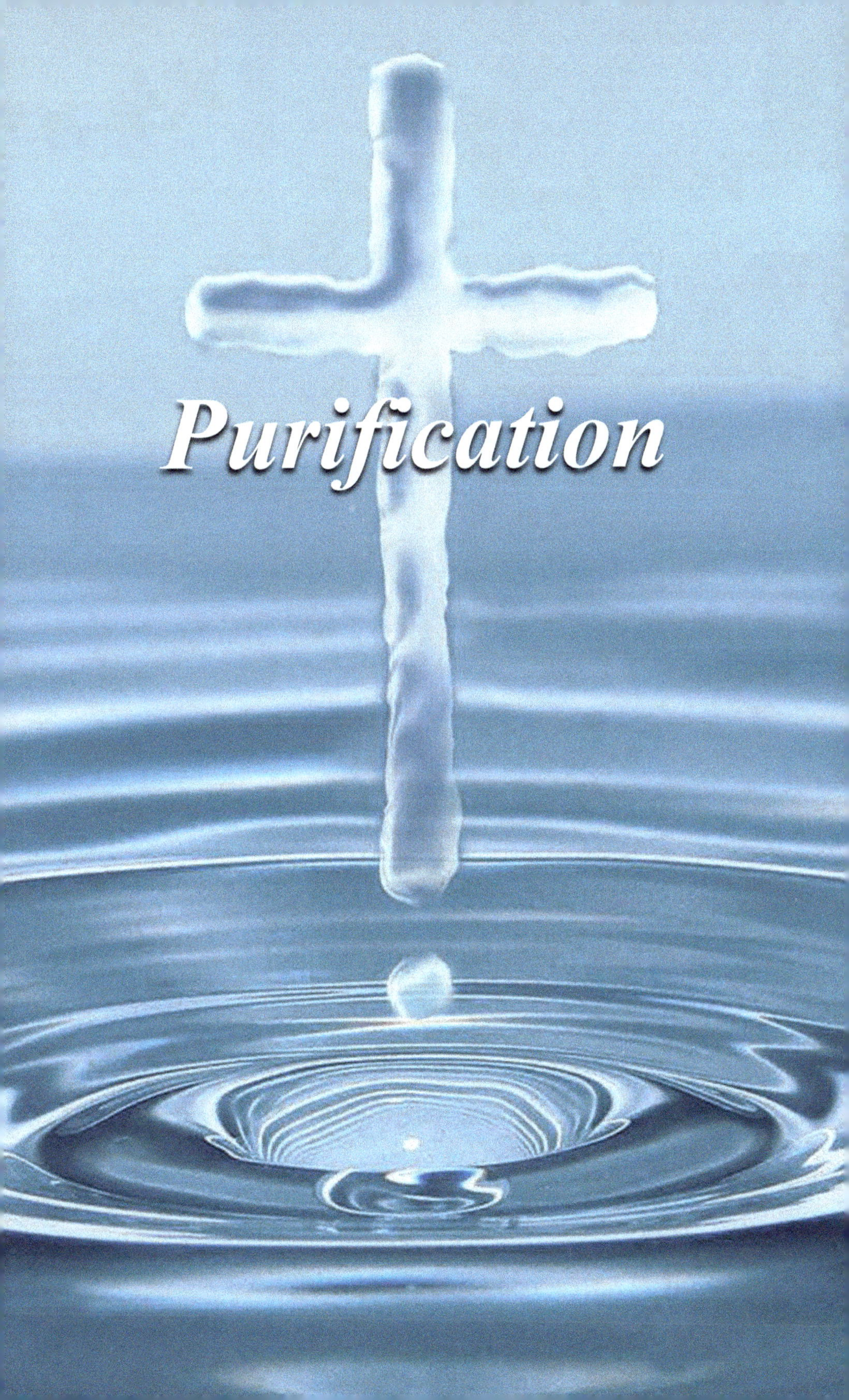
Purification

Chapter 6
Purification from Generational Iniquity & Freedom from Generational Curse

⁵ And at the evening sacrifice I arose up from my heaviness;
and having rent my garment and my mantle,
I fell upon my knees, and spread out my hands
unto the Lord my God, ⁶ And said, O my God,
I am ashamed and blush to lift up my face to thee, my God:
for our iniquities are increased over our head,
and our trespass is grown up unto the heavens.
Ezra 9:5-6 (KJV)

When a person understands their need for a Saviour, they can position themselves for deliverance from the bondage of generational iniquity in the natural and spiritual areas of their lives. God sent His only begotten Son to pay the penalty and remove the craving for sin from all humanity through the death, burial, and resurrection of Jesus Christ (John 3:16; 8:11). As one receives the gift of salvation through Christ Jesus, they are cleansed from the stains of generational iniquities by the Blood of Jesus and spiritually redeemed back into right standing with the authority of God. As a result, they are in a position to break the generational curse and begin the transformation of their soul (mind, will, and emotions) to live out the healthy and productive life promised by God the Father.

Breaking the Curse

God places a curse to bring a person or a family under judgment and therefore to a place where they can receive His mercy and divine forgiveness. This leads to confession, repentance, forgiveness, and freedom. Family weaknesses cause the family to be alienated from the presence of God, creating the need for self-awareness of their moral failure and powerlessness over the nature of sin within themselves. There must be a moment where the family members identify their own behavior in the light of God's Word. The only true deliverance from the generational curse comes from the redemption process of salvation through the finished work of Jesus Christ (crucifixion and resurrection).

> *Christ has redeemed us from the curse of the law,*
> *having become a curse for us (for it is written,*
> *"Cursed is everyone who hangs on a tree"),*
> *Galatians 3:13 (NKJV)*

Though one member of the family unit can advocate for change, each family member (who has reached the age of accountability) is responsible for making their own choice to enter into a personal love relationship with God through Christ to maintain their deliverance.

> [19] *Yet say ye, Why? doth not the son bear the iniquity of the*
> *father? When the son hath done that which is lawful and right,*
> *and hath kept all my statutes, and hath done them,*
> *he shall surely live.* [20] *The soul that sinneth, it shall die.*
> *The son shall not bear the iniquity of the father,*
> *neither shall the father bear the iniquity of the son:*
> *the righteousness of the righteous shall be upon him,*
> *and the wickedness of the wicked shall be upon him.*
> [21] *But if the wicked will turn from all his sins that he hath*

committed, and keep all my statutes, and do that which is
lawful and right, he shall surely live, he shall not die.
[22] All his transgressions that he hath committed,
they shall not be mentioned unto him:
in his righteousness that he hath done he shall live.
Ezekiel 18:19-22 (KJV)

Suppose you are uncertain about the status of your personal relationship with God through His Son Jesus Christ. In that case, I invite you to renew your Kingdom Citizenship with Heaven by praying this Prayer of Salvation.

A PRAYER OF SALVATION

Dear Father, I come to you admitting that I NEED HELP! My heart has been broken, and my spirit has been crushed by trying to solve problems in my own strength. I acknowledge that I am a sinner. Forgive me for my selfish thoughts, bitter feelings, and evil actions. I also choose to forgive myself and others for past hurts, painful actions, and wrong decisions that were made. Lord, I repent by willingly turning away from the desires of my sinful nature and towards the obedience of your life-giving Word.

That if thou shalt confess with thy mouth the Lord Jesus,
and shalt believe in thine heart that God hath raised Him
from the dead, thou shalt be saved
Romans 10:9 (KJV)

Lord, I believe that You sent your Son, Jesus just for me. His death, burial, and resurrection have redeemed me from the death penalty of sin and purchased my salvation into eternal life. The Blood of Jesus has washed and made me clean. I am free! I am saved! I am accepted by You!

¹³ For if ye live after the flesh, ye shall die:
but if ye through the Spirit do mortify
the deeds of the body, ye shall live.
¹⁴ For as many as are led by the Spirit of God,
they are the sons of God.
Romans 8:13-14 (KJV)

Thank you, Father, for welcoming me into the Family of God! I receive the power of Your Holy Spirit to show me how to live my life according to Your divine purpose. I will no longer live with the guilt and shame of my past but in the freedom of Your Holy Spirit. This I pray in Jesus' Name, Amen!

Cleanse Yourself

Pastor King reminds us of the individual responsibility believers have to continue in a life of holiness by cleansing themselves once they have received salvation through Christ Jesus.

> *I'm going to give you a highlight here on the soulish realm. First, we want to read 2 Corinthians 7:1, which I'm reading out of the New King James. It says, "Therefore, having these promises beloved, let us cleanse ourselves from all filthiness of the flesh and spirit perfecting holiness in the fear of God." It is your job to cleanse yourself.*
>
> *[Yet some say] "Oh no, I got the Holy Ghost, Holy Ghost to cleanse me. "*
>
> *It is your job to cleanse your flesh and your spirit. Holy Ghost will help you. Holy Ghost will lead you. Holy Ghost will keep you, but it is your job to cleanse*

> *yourself. It is not your job to come to me to tell me to cleanse you, or for me to come to you for you to cleanse me. You must first make a conscious cognitive well-informed decision that I need to be cleansed. There is a hang-up with the body of Christ, almost as a whole. We do not want to face the fact that we need to be healed. We need to be cleansed. We need to change our mindset, the way we think about things; The very way that we think about things needs to be changed. The mindset needs to be changed. My God, I can feel this thang! Hallelujah, Glory to God!*
>
> *... Pastor Dorene J. King*

It doesn't matter how long you have been saved. We all live in this world and are influenced by the world system. Therefore, we all need to be cleansed from the frustrations of life's routines and purified from the vexations of evil spirits daily.

God's Seed Remains

As Kingdom Citizens, the Holy Spirit will reveal hidden abominations along our journey so we can overcome the attacks of the enemy and continue to live victoriously to the glory of God. As we choose to yield to this process, the seed God has planted will remain and must spring forth.

> *Now because of your nativity, the circumstances surrounding your birth, the devil, everything you birth, the devil wants to be infected. But because the seed remainth in me, I got the victory. So, I may have been birthed with a spiritual disease. I may have been*

birthed out of alcoholism. I may have been birthed out of abortion. You tried to abort me, but I lived on. I may have been birthed out of rejection. I may have been birthed out of adultery. I may have been birthed out of being not wanted, but God's deposit in me remains because God's vein is in me, and it remains. And I am going to be what God has called me to be. No matter how many times I got to get free, I'm going to birth the Godkind of seed out of the seed God put in me. It will overshadow my generational, my ancestry seed. God's seed can wipe out the infection, the pollution, the diseases of your generational seed. Let God wipe out and away everything that was declared over you. Every evil work [and words spoken], "This baby ain't gonna be nothing. You ain't gonna, you ain't, you don't know nothing. You're not smart." Let God overshadow and wipe out every curse, every curse that has been spoken over you.

... Pastor Dorene King

Clean & Pure

How do we cleanse ourselves from generational iniquity, destructive patterns, unhealed hurts, unmet needs, and unresolved issues? First, we must surrender our soul (mind, will, and emotions) to the authority of the Lord God as the Righteous Judge. As we declare His Word through prayers of deliverance with complete confidence and obey His Will, the supernatural power of God is activated and accomplishes His divine purpose in our lives.

Cleansing from Generational Iniquity

As the Holy Spirit reveals the dysfunctional patterns of our past and brings to light the destructive actions of our present, all God desires is that we acknowledge our need for His cleansing, so we may abide in His presence forever.

1. **Recognize and identify** the sin.
2. **Take responsibility and accountability** for committed actions.
3. **Confess and repent** for yourself and on behalf of the family. *(Leviticus 26:40,42; Nehemiah 1:7; 9:2 – Nehemiah repented on behalf of his family line; Israel's Leadership took responsibility for the nation's generational sin).*
4. **Allow God to wash you in the Blood of Jesus Christ** and **accept forgiveness.**

Prophetic Declaration & Prayer

Hallelujah, Lord, we praise you now! As the people sit here and think about the things and their nativity and the circumstances surrounding their very existence in their birth. God, we thank You for Your Blood. And we thank You that Your seed comes in. And as You deposit that in us and we allow it to be released in us, it cleanses us. And You're teaching us how to go and cut the cord. Even from generational curses, even from ancestral evil declarations. Hallelujah, glory! Somebody ought to praise God for that! Hallelujah!

... Pastor Dorene King

PRAYER OF BREAKING SINS & INIQUITIES OF THE FATHERS [20]

I confess the sins and iniquities of my ancestors and my own sin and iniquity of _____.

I release and forgive my ancestors for passing down to me these sins and iniquities and for the resulting curses.

> **Begin forgiving all your ancestors that moved in this sin/iniquity and then anyone who committed this sin against you.*

I repent of this sin and iniquity, and for yielding to it and to the resulting curses. I ask You to forgive me, Lord.

> **Begin to ask God to forgive you for how you have moved in this sin/iniquity against yourself or others.*

I forgive myself for participating in this sin and iniquity.

I renounce the sin and iniquity of _____ and break the power of all resulting curses through the redemptive work of Christ on the Cross and His Shed Blood.

I receive God's freedom from this sin and the resulting curses. Amen!

---

[20] "Prayers for Breaking Sins and Iniquities of the Fathers." *Heaven's Garden Ministries,* Feb. 2018, http://heavensgardenministries.com/wp/wp-content/uploads/2018/02/Prayer-to-Break-Sins-and-Iniquities-of-the-Father.pdf. Accessed 16 Aug 2021

Healing for Unhealed Hurts

He that hath an ear, let him hear what the Spirit saith
unto the churches; To him that overcometh
*will I give to eat of **the tree of life,***
which is in the midst of the paradise of God.
Revelation 2:7 (KJV)

In the midst of the street of it,
*and on either side of the river, was there **the tree of life,***
which bare twelve manner of fruits,
and yielded her fruit every month:
*and the **leaves of the tree were for the healing***
***of the** nations.*
Revelation 22:2 (KJV)

We can abide in Christ, if we allow His Word to abide in us. God sees you through the gracious and forgiving eyes of Christ when you apply His Word to your soul (mind, will, and emotions).

☠ CHANGE YOUR MIND

God wants you to have clarity, a positive self-image, and focus on the precious promises of Christ for your life. This means having a sound mind confident in God's plans and timing, no matter how destructive the fiery situation around you may appear. You must believe that you are entitled to divine healing and restoration through salvation in Christ Jesus.

*Let **this mind** be in you, which was also in **Christ Jesus***:
Philippians 2:5 (KJV)

***For I know the thoughts that I think toward you,** saith the Lord,*
thoughts of peace, and not of evil, to give you an expected end.
Jeremiah 29:11 (KJV)

♥ CONTROL YOUR EMOTIONS

Do not allow fear, anxiety, or worry to rule your heart. Rather than holding on to the stress and strain of the situation, give those negative thoughts and damaging feelings entirely to God and receive His perfect peace that surpasses all understanding, human reasoning, and logic. Exchange the heavy burden of self-induced responsibility for the calming and comforting reassurance that God has handled every obligation. You can find rest and security when your faith is in God's ability to heal and fulfill every promise.

[20] *My son, attend to my words;*
incline thine ear unto my sayings.
[21] *Let them not depart from thine eyes;*
keep them in the midst of thine heart.
[22] *For they are life unto those that find them,*
and health to all their flesh.
[23] **Keep thy heart with all diligence;**
for out of it are the issues of life.
[24] *Put away from thee a froward mouth,*
and perverse lips put far from thee.
[25] *Let thine eyes look right on,*
and let thine eyelids look straight before thee.
[26] *Ponder the path of thy feet, and let all thy ways be established.*
[27] *Turn not to the right hand nor to the left:*
remove thy foot from evil.
Proverbs 4:20-27 (KJV)

And Jesus said unto him,
Go thy way; **thy faith hath made thee whole.**
And immediately he received his sight,
and followed Jesus in the way.
Mark 10:52 (KJV)

🙌 WILLINGLY TAKE GODLY ACTION

Don't make indecisive actions, hasty decisions, or engage in sinful behaviors out of the irritation and tormenting stress of unhealed wounds. Instead, take authority over it by name and ask God to show you the strategic device of the enemy. Bind it and cast it out in Jesus' Name, along with all of its companions, and receive the healing virtue of God. Decree and declare your healing and restoration, then rejoice with a spirit of expectation. Once you have done this, you must choose to allow the forgiveness of God to operate through you and be obedient to the leading of the Holy Spirit, so divine healing can manifest fully in your body, mind, will, and emotions.

> *[30] And do not bring sorrow to God's Holy Spirit by the way you live.*
> *Remember, he has identified you as his own,*
> *guaranteeing that you will be saved on the day of redemption.*
> *[31] **Get rid of all bitterness, rage, anger, harsh words,***
> ***and slander, as well as all types of evil behavior.***
> *[32] Instead, **be kind to each other,***
> ***tenderhearted, forgiving one another,***
> ***just as God through Christ has forgiven you.***
> *Ephesians 4:30-32 (NLT)*

PRAY THE WORD ... HEALING FROM HURT

I bind and cast out every spirit of _____ (name the demonic behavior) and all of its companions that have attacked my spirit, soul, body, and/or _____ (object of the attack) in the name of Jesus. I take authority over the power of the enemy according to the Word of God in Ephesians 1:20-22. I choose to come out from bondage and sin and separate myself unto God! I welcome the spirit of forgiveness, humility, love, joy, peace, patience, kindness, gentleness, faithfulness, self-control, and goodness into my mind, will, and emotions in Jesus' Name. I choose to receive the security and restoration of God that heals my soul and makes it perfectly whole. Lord, thank You for the spirit of wisdom and discernment that will anoint me to accomplish all the things You have purposed me to do in Jesus' Name, Amen.

Provision for all Unmet Needs

---

*I will **open rivers in high places**,
and **fountains in the midst of the valleys**:
I will make the **wilderness a pool of water**,
and the **dry land springs of water**.*
Isaiah 41:18 (KJV)

*Why shouldest thou be as a man astonied,
as a mighty man that cannot save?
yet thou, **O Lord, art in the midst of us**,
and **we are called by thy name; leave us not**.*
Jeremiah 14:9 (KJV)

When we allow our soul to abide in the presence of the Lord, the supernatural provision of God is readily available to respond to the needs that may arise in any area of our lives.

🧠 CHANGE YOUR MIND

Acknowledge that God is the true source of all our daily needs and provision. We must recognize the difference between the desires of our flesh and those needful things that pertain to life and godliness. God will give us the anointing to obtain our needs without toil, stress, or strain.

According as his divine power hath given unto us
all things that pertain unto life and godliness,
through the knowledge of Him
that hath called us to glory and virtue:
2 Peter 1:3 (KJV)

The blessing of the Lord brings wealth, **without painful toil for it.**
Proverbs 10:22 (AMP)

God wants to manifest His heavenly blessings in our lives spiritually, mentally, emotionally, physically, and even financially without any unnecessary struggle, hardship, labor or fatigue.

Also, every man to whom **God has given riches and possessions,**
He has also given the power and ability to enjoy them
and to receive [this as] his [allotted] portion
and to rejoice in his labor— **this is the gift of God** *[to Him].*
Ecclesiastes 5:19 (AMP)

❤ CONTROL YOUR EMOTIONS

In times of financial hardship, when the money gets funny, and the change looks strange, the limited resources do not define who you are, nor should it govern the emotions of your heart. The fear of lack and anxiety of deprivation has no authority over those who are in Christ Jesus. You are not a failure nor a screw-up. These are just opportunities for God to demonstrate His glory by opening doors that you could not even budge in your own strength. So stand in the strength, confidence, and security of God, knowing that He will supply all your needs and prosper you in your purpose.

Allow your heart to rest in the assurance and full confidence of knowing that when you feel you are at your weakest; the strength of God is at work in you to the fullest. The Word of

God tells us in Ephesians 6:10 to be strong in the Lord and power of His might because the power of God is the most effective in human weakness. His grace is sufficient for every situation you may face.

> [9] but He has said to me, "My grace is sufficient for you
> [My lovingkindness and My mercy are more than enough —
> always available —regardless of the situation];
> for [My] power is being perfected [and is completed
> and shows itself most effectively] in [your]weakness.
> " Therefore, I will all the more gladly boast
> in my weaknesses, so that the power of Christ
> [may completely enfold me and] may dwell in me.
> [10] So I am well pleased with weaknesses, with insults,
> with distresses, with persecutions, and with difficulties,
> for the sake of Christ; for when I am weak
> [in human strength], then I am strong [truly able,
> truly powerful, truly drawing from God's strength].
> 2 Corinthians 12:9-10 (AMP)

WILLINGLY TAKE GODLY ACTION

God has anointed you to accomplish all the things that He has purposed you to do. God is not obligated to bless that which He did not sanction, finance our foolish decisions, nor prosper the plans that go against His Will. In other words, He's not paying the bill for an item He did not order. So, you don't need to get upset when your plans, half-brain schemes, or frantic hustles produce little to no profit or success. Instead, repent unto God for yielding to the temptation of pride and selfishness, then renew your trust and faith in God to provide all your needs. Ask God for wisdom, direction, and discernment; then follow His instructions! God's Word works! He will show you how to operate in His provision if you allow yourself to hear His voice and obey His commands.

The young lions do lack, and suffer hunger: but they that seek
the LORD shall not want any good thing.
Psalm 34:10 (KJV)

If the Lord delight in us, then he will bring us into this land,
and give it us; a land which floweth with milk and honey.
Numbers 14:8 (KJV)

Instead of pursuing the creations of God, we are to diligently go after the Creator by developing a relationship with Him through His Son, Jesus Christ, and He will give us the desires of our hearts (Matthew 6:33). The Kingdom of God is not bankrupt, it is rich.

And my God will liberally supply (fill until full) your every
need according to His riches in glory in Christ Jesus.
Philippians 4:19 (AMP)

Let us decree and declare the Word of the Lord in every area of lack or despair in our lives. God has provided every believer with supernatural assistance to usher them into the prepared place He has purposed before the foundations of the world.

*"See, **I am sending an angel before you***
***to protect you** on your journey*
*and **lead you safely to the place I have prepared for you***.
Exodus 23:20 (NLT)

God has provided all the things we need that pertain to life and a lifestyle of holiness. All you have to do is be in a position to receive and utilize the resources of heaven. This includes the angels God has assigned in advance to protect your life and guide you safely to the place God has prepared for you spiritually, physically, mentally, emotionally, and financially. All you have to do is pray the Word of God to activate their assistance as you walk in your divine purpose.

PRAY THE WORD ... MARKETPLACE ANGELS

Lord, I Thank You for Your power and sovereignty over every area of my life. Because I have a relationship with You through Your Son, Jesus Christ, I stand in the authority of Your Word. I declare that wealth and riches are in my house, according to Your Word (Psalm 112:3). Lord, Thank You for sending Your marketplace angels to guard my finances in all areas of business and commercial influence with wisdom, discernment, and care (Matthew 4:6, Luke 4:10). I will humbly walk in the truth and integrity of Your Word concerning all financial transactions that pass through my hands. I will see Your glory revealed and give You praise. In Jesus' Name, Amen.

PRAY THE WORD ... ADMINISTRATIVE ANGELS

Father in the Name of Jesus, I declare the administrative favor of God over every area of my life. I bind the hands of the enemy and cancel every demonic assignment, deceitful agenda, and malicious conversation that would try to hinder the demonstration of God's Glory in my life! Lord, Thank You for sending Your administrative angels to carefully guard and process paperwork, policies, and procedures on my behalf without accident, incident, or delay according to Your Perfect Will. Thank You for anointing me with a spirit of excellence and integrity to accomplish every mandated assignment and designated task You have purposed for me to do. In Jesus' Name, Amen.

Wisdom & Discernment for Unresolved Issues

*But **the natural [unbelieving] man does not accept the things
[the teachings and revelations] of the Spirit of God,***
for they are foolishness [absurd and illogical] to him;
*and **he is incapable of understanding them,***
*because they are **spiritually discerned and appreciated,***
[and he is unqualified to judge spiritual matters].
1 Corinthians 2:14 (AMP)

🧠 CHANGE YOUR MIND

No matter the state of unrest, Jehovah Shalom, the God of Peace, can calm the chaos of the limited carnal mind and bring clarity for those who choose to be spiritually minded by aligning their thoughts with the Word of God. However, God will not go against the established order of His creation or judgments of His Word. Therefore, if we want to receive the insightful revelations God has for our unresolved issues, we must learn to spiritually discern!

*Merriam Webster defines **DISCERNMENT**[21] as:*
- the quality of being able to grasp
and comprehend what is obscure
- an act of perceiving or discerning something

Discernment is the ability to analyze and understand uncertain situations, opportunities, or even people by the wisdom and knowledge of the Holy Spirit. When you are spiritually minded, the indwelling Spirit of God will lead, guide, and direct you in the divine truth concerning every area of your life. This includes the issues surrounding your family, friends, relationships, finances, career, education, etc.

---

[21] "Discernment." Merriam-Webster.com. Merriam-Webster, n.d. Web. 26 Nov. 2018.

That the God of our Lord Jesus Christ,
*the Father of glory, **may give unto you the spirit of wisdom***
***and revelation in the knowledge of Him**:*
Ephesians 1:17 (KJV)

❤ CONTROL YOUR EMOTIONS

If you don't operate in the spirit of forgiveness, you open the door for a greater attack of the enemy. Bitterness, anger, resentment, and unforgiveness do not cultivate a healthy environment for God's divine wisdom and revelation to operate effectively and resolve the issues in your life!

The act of forgiveness places us in right standing with the authority of God. It also allows us to clearly understand the directions of the Holy Spirit and function in wisdom. Therefore, we must let the forgiveness of God operate in every area of our lives by choosing to forgive others and ourselves.

*[14] For **if ye forgive men their trespasses,***
your heavenly Father will also forgive you:
*[15] But **if ye forgive not men their trespasses,***
***neither will your Father forgive your trespasses**.*
Matthew 6:14-15 (KJV)

🙏🙏 WILLINGLY BRING YOURSELF SUBJECT TO GOD'S WORD

When the Spirit of God quiets the internal storms, we must put action to our faith through our obedience to His Word. It will not be comfortable to the flesh to demonstrate the love, peace, and forgiveness of God to those who played a part in our issues.

35 And the same day, when the even was come,
he saith unto them, Let us pass over unto the other side.
36 And when they had sent away the multitude,
they took him even as he was in the ship.
And there were also with him other little ships.
37 And there arose a great storm of wind,
and the waves beat into the ship, so that it was now full.
38 And he was in the hinder part of the ship,
asleep on a pillow: and they awake him, and say unto him,
Master, carest thou not that we perish?
*39 **And he arose, and rebuked the wind,***
and said unto the sea, Peace, be still.
And the wind ceased, and there was a great calm.
*40 And he said unto them, **Why are ye so fearful?***
how is it that ye have no faith?
41 And they feared exceedingly, and said one to another,
What manner of man is this,
that even the wind and the sea obey him?
Mark 4:35-41(KJV)

Just know that there is a divine anointing that is released when we choose to ask, listen and obey the direction of God for our character, conduct, and conversation daily. This means surrendering the responsibility to make things happen by our own strength and relinquishing any self-imposed superiority to God. One must turn away from the self-righteous inclinations of the flesh and choose to complete the assignments of God without question, compromise, or complaining. His divine perspective brings supernatural healing and closure to unresolved issues. His innovative ideas and plans are guaranteed to produce the "God results" of increase, wealth, and honor in every area of our lives.

That ye may be blameless and harmless, the sons of God,
*without rebuke, **in the midst of a crooked and perverse nation**,*
among whom ye shine as lights in the world;
Philippians 2:15 (KJV)

You must make a choice to forgive any negative thought, word, or deed done to you, regardless of how you feel or others respond. The intentional and conscious act of forgiving closes the door to bitterness, pride, and resentment in your heart. It opens the door for the unconditional love, blessings, and forgiveness of God to flow freely in your life. But, conversely, if you do not forgive others, Christ cannot forgive you and reveal His glorious purpose in your life.

PRAY THE WORD ... FORGIVENESS

Lord forgive me for holding on to anger, bitterness, resentment, and strife towards _____ for the decisions and actions they chose to make.

Lord, thank You for forgiving me, and I choose to forgive myself for the actions and decisions that played a part and/or occurred as a result of this situation.

I bind and cast out every spirit of unforgiveness, bitterness, pride, resentment, rejection, and all of its companions that I allowed in my soul and spirit, in Jesus' Name. I am loosed and set free. I choose to let go of the hurt, pain, disappointment, and offense that resulted from their actions, whether knowingly or unknowingly.

I welcome the spirit of forgiveness, humility, love, joy, peace, patience, kindness, gentleness, faithfulness, self-control, and goodness into my mind, will, and emotions in Jesus' Name.

I choose to receive the security and restoration of God that heals my soul and makes it perfectly whole.

I willingly choose to forgive _____.
Lord bless, _____. Let Your lovingkindness minister to their hearts, Your perfect peace overtake their minds, and Your divine wisdom guide them to make good decisions according to Your Word. Usher them into a truly intimate relationship with You. Father prosper, strengthen, empower, and anoint them to accomplish all the things You have purposed them to do. Lord, thank You for showing me how to love them with Your unconditional love. This I pray in Jesus' Name, Amen.

Do not get discouraged. It does not matter how polluted your bloodline may be; God is here to cleanse, heal, and set you free. Even if you fall, again and again, allow the Holy Spirit to pick you up and start anew. God wants to clean you up, shower you with loving care, and give you the Kingdom inheritance He has provided for His children.

> [6] *"And **when I passed by you and saw you <u>struggling in your own Blood</u>, I said to you in your Blood, 'Live!' Yes, I said to you in your Blood, 'Live!'***
> [7] **I made you thrive** like a plant in the field; and **you grew, matured,** and **became very beautiful**. Your breasts were formed, your hair grew, but you were naked and bare.
> [8] "When I passed by you again and looked upon you, **indeed your time was the time of love;** so I spread My wing over you and covered your nakedness. Yes, I swore an oath to you and entered into a covenant with you, and you became Mine," says the Lord God.
> [9] "Then **I washed you in water; <u>yes, I thoroughly washed off your Blood, and I anointed you with oil.</u>***
> Ezekiel 16:6-14 (NKJV)*

Kingdom Heritage

Chapter 7
Reclaim the Kingdom Culture & Family of God

> *The way to reclaim the Kingdom Heritage of God in your life is by making a paradigm shift into God's Kingdom Culture & Family.*

G od's original intent for mankind was to have dominion over the earth according to His kingdom governance and living in the victorious provision of His Glory in every area of our lives (Genesis 1:26 – 30). This includes the prospering of God's Seed in our personal well-being, property, finances, community, ministry, commerce, education, social relationships, and FAMILY LEGACY!

[1]When Abram was ninety-nine years old,
the Lord appeared to him and said,
"I am El-Shaddai—'God Almighty.' Serve me faithfully
and live a blameless life. [2] I will make a covenant with you,
by which I will guarantee to give you countless descendants."
[3] At this, Abram fell face down on the ground.
Then God said to him, [4] "This is my covenant with you:
I will make you the father of a multitude of nations!
[5] What's more, I am changing your name.
It will no longer be Abram. Instead, you will be called Abraham,
for you will be the father of many nations.

⁶ I will make you extremely fruitful. Your descendants will
become many nations, and kings will be among them!
⁷ "I will confirm my covenant with you and your descendants
after you, from generation to generation.
This is the everlasting covenant: I will always be your God
and the God of your descendants after you.
⁸ And I will give the entire land of Canaan,
where you now live as a foreigner, to you and your
descendants. It will be their possession forever,
and I will be their God."
Genesis 17:1-9 (NLT)

The process of deliverance reverses the curse and allows us to release the weakness of family iniquities and reclaim the righteous holiness of the family of God. However, this exchange requires a paradigm shift in the mind of the believer.

> *Defining PARADIGM (Kopp) [22]*
>
> *"The word "paradigm" comes from the Greek. It originally was a scientific term but is more commonly used today to mean a model, theory, perception, assumption or frame of reference. In the general sense, it is the "way we view" the world ... in terms of perceiving, understanding, interpreting.*

As human beings, the framework, or paradigm, determines how we think about situations and respond to our environment in every area of our lives. It is determined by our upbringing and childhood (whether functional or dysfunctional) and tainted by sin and generational iniquity. This faulty framework is built on the foundation of subjective morality, worldly philosophies, and

---

[22] Kopp, Dr. Russell R. "Chapter 1: A New Paradigm for Counseling – What is a Paradigm?" *An Introduction to Family Systems: A Study of the Family as a System and How to Create a Healthy Family System.* Jacksonville: Logos, n.d. Text Book. p. 6.

deceptions, resulting in a shaky construction that is not up to code compared to God's righteous standards and Kingdom truths.

When we allow the Spirit of God to usher us through the process of a paradigm shift, we can build our lives on a sure foundation that can withstand the tests and unexpected hardships of life. It is also a sanctuary of God's provision and peace. This is why we need to put off the old sinful nature of man and its way of thinking (the world system) and put on the Holy nature and mind of Jesus Christ (Philippians 2:5), reclaiming the Kingdom heritage God has established for His children who believe.

> *Defining PARADIGM SHIFT [23]*
> *an important change that happens when the usual way of thinking about or doing something is replaced by a new and different way*

> [21] *Since you have heard about Jesus and have learned the truth that comes from him,* [22] *throw off your old sinful nature and your former way of life, which is corrupted by lust and deception.* [23] *Instead, let the Spirit renew your thoughts and attitudes.* [24] *Put on your new nature, created to be like God—truly righteous and holy.*
> *Ephesians 4:21-24 (NLT)*

As believing Kingdom Citizens who identify with the kingdom culture of Christ Jesus, we are no longer bound by the perverse nature or destructive generational patterns of dysfunctional family belief systems that lead to addictions and violence. Instead, we have been adopted into the Holy Family of God, given a new functional family pattern (the laws of God) and family

---

[23] "Paradigm shift." Merriam-Webster.com Dictionary, Merriam-Webster, https://www.merriam-webster.com/dictionary/paradigm%20shift. Accessed 16 Aug. 2021.

spirit (the Holy Spirit of God) to carry out those laws and steward the inheritance.[24]

> [1]*Everyone who believes that Jesus is the Christ*
> *has become a child of God. And everyone who loves*
> *the Father loves his children, too.* [2] *We know we love*
> *God's children if we love God and obey his commandments.*
> [3] *Loving God means keeping his commandments,*
> *and his commandments are not burdensome.*
> *1 John 5:1-3 (NLT)*

Make the paradigm shift by cognitively changing your actions to reflect God's character, nature, and image.

1. **Close the door on the old dysfunctional ancestral family patterns and generational iniquity.**
2. **Open the door to the new functional Family of God patterns** by meditating and obeying God's Word. *This will prepare you to receive the blessings and steward the inheritance of the Kingdom.*

> [9] *Those who have been born into God's family do not make*
> *a practice of sinning, because God's life is in them.*
> *So they can't keep on sinning, because they are children of God.*
> [10] *So now we can tell who are children of God*
> *and who are children of the devil.*
> *Anyone who does not live righteously*
> *and does not love other believers does not belong to God.*
> *1 John 3:9 – 10 (NLT)*

---

[24] Hawkey, Ruth. "Chapter 11: The Power of the Cross – The Will of God." *Freedom from Generational Sin.* Chichester: New Wine Press, 1999. Book. pgs. 59-60.

Chapter 8
Living the Kingdom Existence

> *Beloved, I wish above all things*
> *that thou mayest prosper and be in health,*
> *even as thy soul prospereth.*
> *3 John 1:2 (KJV)*

Complete wholeness isn't just material. It encompasses your spirit, body, and soul – mind, will, and emotions, **your total well-being.** Operating in the absolute peace of God (Shalom) means allowing Jehovah Rapha (which is the Hebrew name of God meaning *The God Who Heals and Makes Whole*) to usher you to a place of:

- clarity and security in **your mind**;
- joy and contentment in **your heart**;
- and wise direction for **your will** to follow.

It is the believer's responsibility to purposefully abide in the complete peace of God and maintain their deliverance from generational iniquity.

Wholeness Requires Total Transparency

After breaking the curse and receiving the cleansing healing virtue of Christ, if the Kingdom believer is not totally transparent with God through the guidance of the Holy Spirit, they will not be able to operate in Kingdom wholeness. Unrecognized filth and pollution can remain in the soul and open the door to the same destructive patterns they were delivered from. Let us look at the Gospel of Mark's account of *The Woman with the Issue of Blood*.

Mark 5:24-26 (NKJV)

[24] So Jesus went with him, and a great multitude followed Him and thronged Him.
[25] Now a certain woman had a flow of blood for twelve years,
[26] and had suffered many things from many physicians.
She had spent all that she had and was no better, but rather grew worse.

This woman was desperate for things to change in her life. The sickness in her body caused her to suffer physically, mentally, emotionally, financially, and socially. It is said that she had an incurable disease. Therefore, the physicians were overcharging her for elaborate procedures that had no hope of working. This condition made her ceremonially unclean. Consequently, she was shunned by the religious community, rejected by society, and isolated from her family.

Mark 5:27-28 (NKJV)

[27] When she heard about Jesus, she came behind Him in the crowd and touched His garment.
[28] For she said, "If only I may touch His clothes, I shall be made well."

She had heard of Jesus and was so determined to get a resolution for her unresolved issue of blood that she crawled along the muddy ground through a large crowd of smelly feet to get her healing. When she touched the hem of Jesus' garment (most likely grabbing hold of the tassels of His tallit, which were braided cords that represented the Word of God), she declared her healing by reminding God of His Word, that He is Jehovah Rapha, the God Who Heals and Makes Whole.

Mark 5:29 (NKJV)

²⁹ Immediately the fountain of her blood was dried up, and she felt in her body that she was healed of the affliction.

This woman put action to her confession of faith and was immediately healed of the infirmity in her body. Yet, she was still contaminated in her soul. Her mind, will, and emotions were polluted with the disappointment, rejection, anger, betrayal, bitterness, resentment, depression, and unforgiveness of her experiences. The shame and condemnation of her filthy soul caused her to remain hidden among the crowd on the ground.'

Mark 5:30-32 (NKJV)

³⁰ And Jesus, immediately knowing in Himself that power had gone out of Him, turned around in the crowd and said, "Who touched My clothes?"

³¹ But His disciples said to Him, "You see the multitude thronging You, and You say, 'Who touched Me?' "

³² And He looked around to see her who had done this thing.

When Jesus asked, *"Who touched Me?"* He did not ask because He was unaware but because He was extending her an invitation to be transparent about her trauma and expose the infected wounds of her mind, will, and emotions. Jesus said in John 10:30, *"I and my Father are one."* Therefore, He is El Roi, *the God Who Sees Me.* He is familiar with the stench of the sin-sick soul and filthiness of guilt, shame, and condemnation. He came not only to treat the symptom but also to provide the cure, HIMSELF! Jesus saw the woman hiding in her filth and yet wanted to give her the opportunity to not only know of Him but enter into an intimate relationship with Him, the manifested Word of God.

Luke 8:47 (NKJV)

*[47] Now when **the woman saw that she was not hidden**, she came trembling; and falling down before Him, she declared to Him in the presence of all the people the reason she had touched Him and how she was healed immediately.*

Mark 5:33 (NKJV)

*[33] But the woman, fearing and trembling, knowing what had happened to her, came and fell down before Him and told Him **the whole truth**.*

She accepted the invitation and told him the **WHOLE TRUTH!** She lowered the posture of her heart in humility and was transparent with Christ.

Mark 5:34 (KJV)

*[34] And he said unto her, Daughter, **thy faith hath made thee whole**; go in peace, and **be whole** of thy plague.*

Mark 5:34 (NLT)

---

[34] *And he said to her, "Daughter, your faith has made you well. Go in peace. **Your suffering is over.**"*

Now she was made **entirely whole** in her spirit, soul, and body. Her suffering was over! She was no longer "the woman with the issue of blood" but the "Daughter" who is accepted into the Kingdom Family of God and covered by the Blood of Jesus.

Her journey to maintaining deliverance began with the cognitive decision and intentional choice to be transparent with Christ Jesus in the other hidden areas of her life and surrender to His Divine Will.

Practical Strategies for Kingdom Wholeness

God has provided practical applications of His Word to maintain spiritual deliverance and support for the natural process of recovery that is not centered on guilt, shame, or condemnation. As a result, there is a hope of transforming the family system from dysfunctional bondage to healthy and thriving in the freedom of Christ.

The twelve steps listed are designed to show a lifestyle recovery plan using related scriptures from the Book of Romans.[25]

---

[25]*Adapted from* "The Romans Road to Recovery" by Kopp, Dr. Russell R. "Chapter 12: CO-DEPENDENCE" *Addiction, Intervention, & Recovery.* Jacksonville: Logos, n.d. Text Book. p.124.

- **Step One: Realize that we all have generational iniquity and dysfunctional habits.** *Acknowledging the secret sins and faults unto God is not a sign of weakness or shame, but honesty and humility.*

Romans 1:16, 21, 24 (KJV)

[16] For I am not ashamed of the gospel of Christ:
for it is the power of God unto salvation to every one that believeth;
to the Jew first, and also to the Greek.

[21] Because that, when they knew God, they glorified him not as
God, neither were thankful; but became <u>vain in their</u>
<u>imaginations</u>, and <u>their foolish heart was darkened</u>.

[24] Wherefore God also gave them up to uncleanness
through the lusts of their own hearts,
to dishonour their own bodies between themselves:

- **Step Two: Remove the blinders and identify** the family flaws, weaknesses, and destructive tendencies.

Romans 2:16 (KJV)

[16] In the day when God shall judge <u>the secrets of men</u> by Jesus
Christ according to my gospel.

Proverbs 28:13 (KJV)

[13] <u>He that covereth his sins shall not prosper</u>:
but <u>whoso confesseth and forsaketh them shall have mercy</u>.

- **Step Three: Reaffirm your helplessness.** *We cannot live prosperous and productive lives outside the presence of the Creator, nor can we handle the full weight of sin and its consequences. We need help!*

Romans 3:20 (KJV)

²⁰ Therefore by the deeds of the law there shall <u>no flesh be justified in his sight:</u> for by the law is the knowledge of sin.

- **Step Four: Recognize the power of faith.** *Even though you may not presently see the productive life God has predestined for you, it is available to you now. Therefore, trust and believe in God's vision for your life.*

Romans 4:17 (KJV)

¹⁷ (As it is written, I have made thee a father of many nations,) before him whom he believed, even God, who quickeneth the dead, and <u>calleth those things which be not as though they were.</u>

- **Step Five: Receive God's Unconditional Love.** *Nothing can disqualify us from God's love if we choose to receive it. The merciful Blood of Jesus Christ places us in right standing with the authority of God, quiets the accusations of the enemy, and saves us from the guilt of sin and wrath of God.*

Romans 5:8-9 (KJV)

⁸ But <u>God commendeth his love toward us,</u> in that, while we were yet sinners, Christ died for us. ⁹ Much more then, <u>being now justified by his Blood, we shall be saved from wrath through him.</u>

- **Step Six: Relinquish self-ownership to God.** *Allow God to be your Lord and Master. By freely choosing to comply with His Will, the actions of your mind, will, emotions, and body will be in good standing in the authority of God.*

Romans 6:13 (KJV)

[13] Neither yield ye your members as instruments of unrighteousness unto sin: but <u>yield yourselves unto God</u>, as those that are alive from the dead, and <u>your members as instruments of righteousness unto God</u>.

- **Step Seven: Return to truthful thinking** *(allow your mind to operate according to the truth of God's Word)*, **healthy emotions** *(do not allow your feelings to operate in fear and rejection, but the acceptance and security of the Heavenly Father)*, and **responsible behavior** *(the actions of your will should honor and respect the character, nature, and sovereign authority of God, the Creator of all things).*

Romans 7:23 (KJV)

[23] But I see another law in my members, warring against <u>the law of my mind</u>, and bringing me into captivity to the law of sin which is in my members.

Romans 8:14-16 (KJV)

[14] For as many as are led by the Spirit of God, they are the sons of God.
[15] For ye have not received the spirit of bondage again to fear;

but ye have received <u>the Spirit of adoption</u>,
whereby we cry, Abba, Father.

[16] The Spirit itself beareth witness with our spirit,
that we are the children of God:

Romans 9:20-21 (KJV)

[20] Nay but, O man, <u>who art thou that repliest against God?</u>
Shall the thing formed say to <u>him that formed it</u>,
Why hast thou made me thus?
[21] Hath not the potter power over the clay,
of the same lump to make one vessel unto honour,
and another unto dishonour?

- **Step Eight: Routinely take a personal inventory of your actions and perform an intensive internal audit.** *Remain humble enough to recognize that you cannot sustain daily righteousness living in your own strength. If you fall, Jesus is the advocate that can cleanse and restore you.*

Romans 10:9-11 (KJV)

[9] That if thou shalt confess with thy mouth the Lord Jesus,
and shalt believe in thine heart
that God hath raised him from the dead, thou shalt be saved.
[10] For with the heart man believeth unto righteousness;
and with the mouth confession is made unto salvation.
[11] For the scripture saith, <u>Whosoever believeth on him</u>
<u>shall not be ashamed</u>.

- **Step Nine: Restore broken relationships.** *(The kindness and sternness of God can see the true intents of men's hearts and repair damaged relationships back to His original plan & purpose if they are willing.)*

Romans 11:22-23 (KJV)

[22] *Behold therefore <u>the goodness and severity of God</u>:
on them which fell, severity; but toward thee,
goodness, if thou continue in his goodness:
otherwise thou also shalt be cut off.* [23] *And they also,
if they abide not still in unbelief, shall be grafted in:
for <u>God is able to graft them in again</u>.*

- **Step Ten: Replace one's lifestyle.** *As new creatures in Christ Jesus, we must stop old destructive habits and cultivate a new way of living that places the truth and goodness of God as the first priority in every area of our lives.*

Romans 12:1-2, 9 (KJV)

[1] *I beseech you therefore, brethren, by the mercies of God,
that ye <u>present your bodies a living sacrifice,
holy, acceptable unto God,
which is your reasonable service</u>.
[2] And <u>be not conformed to this world:
but be ye transformed by the renewing of your mind</u>,
that ye may prove what is that good,
and acceptable, and perfect, will of God.*

[9] <u>*Let love be without dissimulation.*
Abhor that which is evil; cleave to that which is good</u>.

- **Step Eleven: Relieve other's burdens.** *We can remove the burdens of injustice, pain, anxiety, bitterness, or resentment from others by being respectful and demonstrating God's grace and lovingkindness in daily routines.*

Romans 13:9-10 (KJV)

⁹ For this, Thou shalt not commit adultery,
Thou shalt not kill, Thou shalt not steal,
Thou shalt not bear false witness, Thou shalt not covet;
and if there be any other commandment,
it is briefly comprehended in this saying,
namely, <u>Thou shalt love thy neighbour as thyself</u>.
¹⁰ <u>Love worketh no ill to his neighbour: therefore love is the fulfilling of the law</u>.

- **Step Twelve: Reach out to others.** *God designed the Body of Christ to be a community of believers that can peacefully support, encourage, and strengthen one another in their spiritual growth by the love and power of His Holy Spirit.*

Romans 14:15-17 (KJV)

¹⁵ But <u>if thy brother be grieved</u> with thy meat,
<u>now walkest thou not</u> charitably.
<u>Destroy not him</u> with thy meat, for whom Christ died.
¹⁶ Let not then your good be evil spoken of:
¹⁷ For <u>the Kingdom of God is</u> not meat and drink;
but <u>righteousness, and peace, and joy in the Holy Ghost</u>.

As we follow the direction of God's Word to maintain our deliverance, we transform our minds and cultivate our hearts to be good stewards over the resources and manifested blessings of God's Kingdom.

> *And be not conformed to this world: but be ye transformed by the renewing of your mind, that ye may prove what is that good, and acceptable, and perfect, will of God.*
> *Romans 12:2 (KJV)*

The Kingdom Life

Kingdom Living means intentionally developing an authentic relationship with Jesus Christ as Savior, Lord, and King. This requires a commitment to hear and obey the commandments of God daily in every area of our lives. It is the decision to choose humility over pride, honesty over lies, even when it's inconvenient or presents a threat of retaliation. It also means wanting to be trustworthy rather than deceitful in the workplace, even if you are not recognized for your achievements or productivity. Finally, it may be the choice between demonstrating loving-kindness or bitter resentment towards family members who have displeased you. Understand that the Holy Spirit will lead, guide, and direct you according to the truth of God's Word. But you must choose to follow the instructions. Don't sabotage yourself by choosing actions that go outside the integrity and truth of God's Word (Romans 8:1 – 17).

> [5] *For they that are after the flesh do mind the things of the flesh; but they that are after the Spirit the things of the Spirit.*
> [6] *For to be carnally minded is death; but to be spiritually minded is life and peace.*
> *Romans 8:5 – 6 (KJV)*

¹⁸ "Come now, let us settle the matter,"
says the Lord.
"Though your sins are like scarlet,
they shall be as white as snow;
though they are red as crimson,
they shall be like wool.
¹⁹ If you are willing and obedient,
you will eat the good things of the land;
²⁰ but if you resist and rebel,
you will be devoured by the sword."
For the mouth of the Lord has spoken.
Isaiah 1:18-20 (NIV)

God the Father generously provides for all the needs of His children. The glory of a king is seen and measured in the lavish provision of his subjects and kingdom. Therefore, God, the King of Glory, wants His children to reflect His beauty and splendor as rightful heirs to the Kingdom. He sustains those who choose to stay in a relationship with Him through Christ Jesus.

*And **my God will liberally supply (fill to the full) your every need** according to His riches in glory in Christ Jesus.*
Philippians 4:19 (AMPC)

*¹⁰ **I clothed you in embroidered cloth**
and **gave you sandals of badger skin;**
I clothed you with fine linen and **covered you with silk**.*

*¹¹ **I adorned you with ornaments**,
put bracelets on your wrists, and **a chain on your neck**.*

*¹² And **I put a jewel in your nose, earrings in your ears,
and a beautiful crown on your head**.*

POLLUTED IN YOUR OWN BLOOD

*13 Thus **you were adorned with gold and silver,
and your clothing was of fine linen,
silk, and embroidered cloth.**
You ate pastry of fine flour, honey, and oil.
You were exceedingly beautiful, and succeeded to royalty.*

*14 **Your fame went out among the nations
because of your beauty,***
for <u>it was perfect through My splendor</u>
<u>whichT hadbe stowedon y ou,"say sth eLord God.</u>

Ezekiel 16:10 – 14 (NKJV)

CONCLUSION

All of humanity has a polluted bloodline. It is infected with sin, shame, guilt, perverse judgments, and condemnation of the enemy. This tainted blood breeds strife, division, contempt, bitterness, rejection, and rebellion in how we think and treat ourselves and others. These patterns of dysfunction and sinful behaviors spread from one generation to the next. As a result, generational iniquity gives birth to generational curses that open the door for demonic influences and destructive actions continuing to the third and fourth generations (Exodus 34:7). This can manifest in a continual lack of living resources, emotional wounds, and traumatic hardships that hinder the possibility of a viable life, much like an abandoned newborn infant struggling in its own polluted blood. But there is hope! God has provided a cure for the curse and cleansing for the pollution.

Christ purchased our freedom [redeeming us]
from the curse (doom) of the Law [and its condemnation]
by [Himself] becoming a curse for us,
for it is written [in the Scriptures],
Cursed is everyone who hangs on a tree (is crucified);

Galatians 3:13 (AMPC)

POLLUTED IN YOUR OWN BLOOD

We can reclaim the Kingdom Heritage of Christ Jesus. One must choose to maintain deliverance by cultivating a relationship with God and complying with the Kingdom strategies of His Word. We will then experience the security and fellowship of God's functional family system and operate in the glorious provision He has pre-ordained for each of His covenant relationship children.

And when I passed by thee,
*and saw thee **polluted in thine own blood**,*
I said unto thee when thou wast in thy blood,
Live; yea, I said unto thee
when thou wast in thy blood, Live.

Ezekiel 16:6 (KJV)

ABOUT THE AUTHOR

I'm Dr. Miracle Pettenger and I teach women how to fight the frustrations and calm the chaos of life experiences, so they can live in the grace and anointing of God.

Miracle Pettenger is a wife, mother, author, speaker, and ordained Apostle with over 25 years of ministry experience. She is the Founder and serves as Pastor of Proceeding Word Apostolic Ministries, Inc., a local ministry in Virginia Beach, VA, that teaches God's proceeding plans and promises for victorious living.

Holding a Bachelor of Arts Degree in Math/Computer Science and Master of Science Degree in Information Systems Management with 14 years of corporate implementation, Dr. Miracle provides logistical management and business services as owner & operator of MP2XEVENTS LLC.

She is also the executive producer of The Miracle Connection, a TV-rated Christian Broadcast that shares biblical teachings and practical strategies for Kingdom Living in Christ Jesus.

Her Doctoral Degree in Theological Studies from Regency

Christian College in Jacksonville, FL supports her mission to bring healing, deliverance, and hope through practical biblical tools that encourage a positive self-image while operating in God's Kingdom principles and divine purpose.

For more books, audio podcasts, inspirational videos, and purpose devotionals by Dr. Miracle Pettenger, please visit
www.miraclepettenger.com

In Loving Memory

Dorene J. Mills was born in June of 1955 and graduated from Octorara High School in Atglen, PA. After which, she served in the U.S. Army, where she met her husband Bishop Joseph King of 35 years. Apostle King graduated from Rhema Seminary and College in Norfolk, Virginia, with her Bachelor of Arts Degree in Biblical Studies. She graduated from Norfolk Seminary and College in Norfolk, VA, with her Master's Degree in Divinity. Her desire was to complete her Doctorate Degree in Theological Studies and Divinity.

Apostle D.J. King, along with her husband, was a founder, pastor, and overseer of New Beginnings Apostolic Faith Ministries, Inc of Virginia Beach, VA. The Lord blessed them with one daughter and one son.

Her goal of taking the Kingdom of God to the people, according to Mark 16:12 – 20, by teaching the practical application of the Word for daily living was fulfilled through televised bible studies, deliverance workshops, prison outreach, and international evangelism.

Apostle King lived a saved and Holy Ghost-filled life for nearly 40 years and transitioned peacefully to glory on January 28, 2012. She would often proclaim, "*God's Word is true. It has the power within itself, to bring itself to past.*"

"Change only comes in the presence of the Lord!"
~ Apostle Dorene J. King

www.ingramcontent.com/pod-product-compliance
Lightning Source LLC
Chambersburg PA
CBHW070829100426
42813CB00003B/542